THROUGH THE EYES OF
C.H. SPURGEON

THROUGH THE EYES OF
C.H. SPURGEON

EDITED BY
STEPHEN McCASKELL

FOREWORD BY
TIM CHALLIES

FREE GRACE PRESS

Through the Eyes of C. H. Spurgeon

Free Grace Press
1076 Harkrider
Conway, AR 72032
freegracepress.com

ISBN: 978-1-952599-08-8

Acknowledgments

Thank you to all who helped this book become a reality. A special thanks to Curt Arend, Tyler Horton, Jeff Landon, Keith and Merrylin McCaskell, Samantha McCaskell, Deitric Newman, Tom Newman, Jeff and Jennifer de Ruyter, Benjamin West, and Luke Wilson.

Contents

Foreword

There are some people, a very select number, who stand apart from the rest of us by their sheer quotability. Winston Churchill, Mark Twain, and William Shakespeare were each able to use words with such skillful economy that today they are known as much for what they said as what they did. There are some Christians who are equally quotable and equally skilled in using language in such a way that great truths are compacted into few words. As a lover of words and a lover of quotes, I often turn to C. S. Lewis, G. K. Chesterton, and Matthew Henry, among others. Here are Christians who could gather the great truths of Scripture and distill them to their very essence.

Perhaps no Christian was more adept at turning a phrase than Charles Haddon Spurgeon. Certainly no Christian has been more quotable than the Prince of Preachers. Sometimes with dead earnest and sometimes with cutting wit, Spurgeon would often summarize an entire section of a sermon or an entire chapter of a book with one small quote, a few words, or a couple of sentences.

A prolific preacher and author, Spurgeon's sermons alone fill some sixty-three volumes; his books and other writings fill many more than that. In *Through the Eyes of C. H. Spurgeon*, Stephen McCaskell has compiled thousands of Spurgeon's punchiest and most powerful quotes and has helpfully categorized them. Here the reader will find wisdom that extends from *acceptance* to *work* and everything in between. Here the reader will find quotes that merit thought, reflection, and attention. They are like hard candy—better savored than quickly chewed and swallowed. Read this book to generate thought and reflection. Read it to find the perfect quote for your book or sermon or blog post. Read it, and I am certain you will be blessed.

Tim Challies - Pastor of Grace Fellowship Church, blogger,
author of *The Next Story*, *Sexual Detox*, and *Visual Theology*

Acceptance

God is so boundlessly pleased with Jesus that in him he is altogether well pleased with us.

Accepted of the Great Father,
Volume 29, Sermon #1731 - Ephesians 1:6

Afflictions

Affliction hardens those whom it does not soften.

The Heart of Flesh,
Volume 19, Sermon #1129 - Ezekiel 36:26

Some of you people of God, when you get bitter waters, want to throw them away. Do not throw a drop of it away, for that is the water you have yet to drink. Accept your afflictions. They are a part of your education.

Marah Better Than Elim,
Volume 39, Sermon #2301 - Exodus 15:22-26

All afflictions are not chastisements for sin; there are some afflictions that have quite another end and object.

God's Works Made Manifest,
Volume 39, Sermon #2309 - John 9:3

Alcohol

The best way to make a man sober is to bring him to the foot of the cross.

An All Around Ministry, Page 108

I abstain myself from alcoholic drink in every form, and I think others would be wise to do the same; but of this each one must be a guide unto himself.

The Waterpots at Cana,
Volume 26, Sermon #1556 - John 2:7

Go not to wine for comfort in the hour of depression. Above all things, dread the intoxicating cup in all its forms.

The Best Strengthening Medicine,
Volume 37, Sermon #2209 - Hebrews 11:34

It is a merciful thing that God forgives drunkenness. Some of those who have wallowed in it have been saved.

God's Firebrands,
Volume 57, Sermon #3233 - Zechariah 3:2

It is the devil's backdoor to hell, and everything that is hellish; for he that once gives away his brains to drink is ready to be caught by Satan for anything.

God's Firebrands,
Volume 57, Sermon #3233 - Zechariah 3:2

Angels

If you had eyes to see, you would perceive a bodyguard of angels always attending every one of the blood-bought family.

Words of Cheer, Page 30

If two angels were sent down to earth, one to rule an empire, and the other to sweep a street, they would have no choice in the matter, so long as God ordered them.

Words of Cheer, Page 50

The angels in heaven are humble because they remember who made them and kept them angels, for they would have been devils in hell if God had not preserved them in their first estate.

It Pleased God,
Volume 56, Sermon #3202 - Galatians 1:15

The angels will know their Master's property. They know each saint, for they were present at his birthday.

What in the Barn,
Volume 60, Sermon #3393 - Matthew 13:30

Anger

Anger is a short madness. The less we do when we go mad the better for everybody, and the less we go mad the better for ourselves.

John Ploughman's Pictures, Page 36

Do nothing when you are out of temper, and then you will have the less to undo.

John Ploughman's Pictures, Page 37

Anger does a man more hurt than that which made him angry.

John Ploughman's Pictures, Page 37

People look none the handsomer for being red in the face.

John Ploughman's Pictures, Page 144

Remember, anger is temporary insanity.

Christ's People – Imitators of Him,
Volume 1, Sermon #21 - Acts 4:13

But oh, beloved, I have no more right as a Christian to suffer bad temper to dwell in me than I have to suffer the devil himself to dwell there.

Secret Sins Driven Out by Stinging Hornets,
Volume 12, Sermon #673 - Deuteronomy 7:20

Fighting sheep are strange animals, and fighting Christians are self-evident contradictions.

Sheep Among Wolves,
Volume 23, Sermon #1370 - Matthew 10:16

Do not say, "I cannot help having a bad temper." Friend, you must help it. Pray God to help you to overcome it at once; for either you must kill it, or it will kill you. You cannot carry a bad temper into heaven.

The Eye and the Light,
Volume 35, Sermon #2109 - Luke 11:33-36

I heard one say that he was sorry that he had lost his temper. I was uncommonly glad to hear that he had lost it, but I regretted that he found it again so soon.

Why Some Seekers Are Not Saved,
Volume 41, Sermon #2411 - Isaiah. 59:1, 2

Little pots soon boil over; and I have known some professing Christians, who are such very little pots, that the smallest fire has made them boil over. When you never meant anything to hurt their feelings, they have been terribly hurt. The simplest remark has been taken as an insult, and a construction put upon things that never was intended, and they make their brethren offenders for a word, or for half a word, ay, and even for not saying a word.

The Third Beatitude,
Volume 53, Sermon #3065 - Matthew 5:5

You have offended God and he is angry. This is not my word: it is written here—"He is angry with the wicked every day. If he turn not, he will whet his sword. He has bent his bow and made it ready." You are in the hands of the God whom you have offended.

The Unfailing Help,
Volume 55, Sermon #3162 - 2 Kings 6:27

Animals

Mr. Rowland Hill used to say that a man was not a true Christian if his dog and his cat were not the better off for it. That witness is true.

First Things First,
Volume 31, Sermon #1864

I do not believe in the piety of a man who is cruel to a horse. There is need of the whip sometimes, but the man who uses it cruelly cannot surely be a converted man.

The Fifth Beatitude,
Volume 55, Sermon #3158 - Matthew 5:7

Treat all creatures kindly, then, so far as you can, for the great Creator's sake.

Christ the Creator,
Volume 56, Sermon #3180 - Colossians 1:16

Argument

Reason is folly with the unreasonable.

John Ploughman's Pictures, Page 58

Some people like rows—I don't envy their choice; I'd rather walk ten miles to get out of a dispute than half-a-mile to get into one.

John Ploughman's Talk, Page 73

Satan greatly approves of our railing at each other, but God does not.

Working Out What Is Worked In,
Volume 14, Sermon #820

Arminianism

I believe it is a mistake about God himself which has been the root and foundation of all the mistakes in theology. Our conviction is, that Arminian theology, to a great extent, makes God to be less than he is.

Even So, Father,
Volume 7, Sermon #394 - Matthew 11:25, 26.

The basis and groundwork of Arminian theology lies in attaching undue importance to man, and giving God rather the second place than the first.

The Infallibility of God's Purpose,
Volume 7, Sermon #406 - Job 23:13

I believe that very much of current Arminianism is simply ignorance of gospel doctrine; and if people began to study their

Bibles, and to take the Word of God as they find it, they must inevitably, if believers, rise up to rejoice in the doctrines of grace.

Knowledge Commended,
Volume 11, Sermon #609 - Daniel 11:32, 33

Atonement

I do not believe in an atonement which is admirably wide, but fatally ineffectual.

Barbed Arrows, Page 143

I may be called Antinomian or Calvinist for preaching a limited atonement; but I had rather believe a limited atonement that is efficacious for all men for whom it was intended, than a universal atonement that is not efficacious for anybody, except the will of man be joined with it.

The Death of Christ,
Volume 4, Sermon #173 - Isaiah 53:10

Once again, if it were Christ's intention to save all men, how deplorably has he been disappointed!

The Mission of the Son of Man(Particular Redemption),
Volume 4, Sermon #204 - Luke 19:10

Never has there been a sin pardoned, absolutely and without atonement, since the world began

Justice Satisfied,
Volume 5, Sermon #255 - Romans 3:26, 1 John 1:9

What the sun is to the heavens, that the doctrine of a vicarious satisfaction is to theology. Atonement is the brain and spinal cord of Christianity. Take away the cleansing blood, and what is left to the guilty? Deny the substitutionary work of Jesus, and you have denied all that is precious in the New Testament.

Grace - The One Way of Salvation,
Volume 13, Sermon #765 - Acts 15:11

To deny the great doctrine of atonement by the blood of Jesus Christ is to hamstring the gospel, and to cut the throat of Christianity.

Is It Nothing to You?,
Volume 27, Sermon #1620 - Lamentations 1:12

I can truly declare among you that I do not preach this doctrine of vicarious sacrifice as one among many theories, but the saving fact of my experience. I must preach this or nothing.

Behold the Lamb of God,
Volume 33, Sermon #1987 - John 1:29

He did not die to make men savable, but to save them.

The Blood of the Lamb, The Conquering Weapon,
Volume 34, Sermon #2043 - Revelation 12:11

We do not believe in a universal redemption which extends even to those who were in hell before the Savior died, and which includes the fallen angels as well as unrepentant men.

Christ's Love for His Vineyard,
Volume 48, Sermon #2785 - Song of Solomon 8:12

I know there is a general aspect to redemption, which brings some good things to all men; but there is also the special aspect in it, which brings all good things to some men.

Trials Expected and Conquered,
Volume 50, Sermon #2877 - Isaiah 43:2, 3

Christ did not die for Judas as he did for Peter; he did not shed his blood for Demas as he shed it for Paul.

God Comforting His People,
Volume 52, Sermon #3012 - Isaiah 49:13

Unless God can undeify himself, every soul that Christ died for he will have.

The Blood of the Testament,
Volume 58, Sermon #3293 - Hebrews 9:19, 20

Baptists

We Baptists like water because our Master has ordained the use of it; but we must also have fire, fire from heaven, the fire of the Holy Ghost.

The Tender Grapes,
Volume 42, Sermon #2480 - Song of Solomon 2:13

I recollect my mother saying to me, "I prayed that you might be a Christian, but I never prayed that you might be a Baptist;" but, nevertheless, I became a Baptist, for, as I reminded her, the Lord was able to do for her exceeding abundantly above what she had asked or thought, and he did it.

The Church - The World's Hope,
Volume 51, Sermon #2952 - Acts 27:24

Beauty

There is little virtue in the beauty which calls attention to itself; modest beauty is the last to extol its own charms.

An All Around Ministry, Page 212

As for beauty, one of its most potent charms lies in its modest unconsciousness; it is greatly marred when accompanied by vanity.

A Catechism for the Proud,
Volume 24, Sermon #1392 - 1 Corinthians 4:7

But men fight against God with God's own gifts. A woman endowed with beauty, the rare gift of God, uses it to ensnare others into sin. God gives us garments, and there are some who use their very garments for nothing else but pride, and who go through the world with no motive but display.

The Unknown Giver and the Misused Gifts,
Volume 38, Sermon #2252 - Hosea 2:8, 9

Belief

Believing is a matter of the will. A man does not believe without being willing to believe.

No Fixity Without Faith,
Volume 39, Sermon #2305 - Isaiah 7:9

If you would believe, your belief will kill your sinning, or else you sinning will kill your believing. The greatest argument against the Bible is an unholy life; and when a man will give that up, he will convince himself.

No Fixity Without Faith,
Volume 39, Sermon #2305 - Isaiah 7:9

The Bible

Never be afraid of your Bibles.

Barbed Arrows, Page 175

The Bible in the memory is better than the Bible in the book case.

Barbed Arrows, Page 279

No parable teaches all sides of truth.

A Good Start, Page 141

Old-fashioned believers could give you chapter and verse for what they believed; but how few of such remain!

The Greatest Fight in the World, Page 45

There is enough dust on some of your Bibles to write "damnation" with your fingers.

The Bible,
Volume 1, Sermon #15 - Hosea 8:12

If you hear a man rail at the Bible, you can usually conclude that he never reads it.

The Spies,
Volume 4, Sermon #197 - Numbers 13:32; 14:6, 7

Nobody ever outgrows scripture; the Book widens and deepens with our years.

The Talking Book,
Volume 17, Sermon #1017 - Proverbs 6:22

The best interpreter of a book is generally the man who wrote it. The Holy Ghost wrote the Scriptures. Go to him to get their meaning, and you will not be misled.

The Secret Food and the Public Name,
Volume 18, Sermon #1079 - Jeremiah 15:16

In the Old Testament we get the facts; in the New Testament we find the explanation of the facts.

Thinking and Turning,
Volume 20, Sermon #1181 - Psalm 119:59

I speak most plainly here, no additional revelation is to be expected, because the book of God is ended, the revelation of God is finished, and he that adds to the sacred book is cursed.

The True Position of the Witness Within,
Volume 24, Sermon #1428 - 1 John 5:10

If you wish to know God you must know his word; if you wish to perceive his power you must see how he works by his word; if you wish to know his purpose before it is actually brought to pass you can only discover it by his word.

The Swiftly Running Word,
Volume 27, Sermon #1607 - Psalms 147:15

The coin of inspiration comes from the mint of infallibility.

Grappling Irons,
Volume 30, Sermon #1779 - Psalm 119:88

Now, mark this: by this shall you know whether you are a child of God, or not; by the respect that you have to your Father's Word. If you have small respect for that Word, the evidences of a bastard are upon you.

A Lesson and a Fortune for Christian Men of Business,
Volume 32, Sermon #1880 - Hebrews 13:5

I have often told you, my dear friends, that I view the difficulties of Holy Scripture as so many prayer-stools upon which I kneel and worship the glorious Lord. What we cannot comprehend by our understandings we apprehend by our affections.

The Lover of God's Law Filled with Peace,
Volume 34, Sermon #2004 - Psalm 119:165

Do we need to understand everything? Are we to be all brain, and no heart? What should we be the better if we did understand all mysteries? I believe God. I bow before his Word. Is not this better for us than the conceit of knowing and understanding? We are as yet mere children. We know in part.

The Lover of God's Law Filled with Peace,
Volume 34, Sermon #2004 - Psalm 119:165

To me the Bible is not God, but it is God's voice, and I do not hear it without awe.

The Word A Sword,
Volume 34, Sermon #2010 - Hebrews 4:12

It is not the book that is to be altered: our hearts want altering.

The Trial of Your Faith,
Volume 34, Sermon #2055 - 1 Peter 1:7

These words come from him who can make no mistake, and who can have no wish to deceive his creatures. If I did not believe in the infallibility of the Book, I would rather be without it. If I am to judge the Book, it is no judge of me.

The Bible Tried and Proved,
Volume 35, Sermon #2084 - Psalm 12:6

The saddest story of Holy Scripture is a beacon, and never a lure.

The Bible Tried and Proved,
Volume 35, Sermon #2084 - Psalm 12:6

The Bible never gives unrenewed human nature a good word, nor does it deserve it.

Pleading, Not Contradicting,
Volume 36, Sermon #2129 - Matthew 15:27

I am perfectly satisfied myself to believe what he writes to me; and if it be so written in his Book, it seems to me to be quite as true and sure as if he had actually come from heaven, and had talked with me, or had appeared to me in the visions of the night.

A Gracious Dismissal,
Volume 37, Sermon #2183 - Luke 7:50

I would rather speak five words out of this book than fifty thousand words of the philosophers.

Come From the Four Winds, O Breath!,
Volume 38, Sermon #2246 - Ezekiel 37:9

It was God's word that made us; is it any wonder that his word should sustain us?

The Best Christmas Fare,
Volume 39, Sermon #2340 - Psalm 119:103

Study the Word, that your faith may not stand in the wisdom of men, but in the power of God!

The Incomparable Bridegroom and His Bride,
Volume 42, Sermon #2469 - Song of Solomon 5:9

Be walking Bibles.

Declaring the Works of the Lord,
Volume 43, Sermon #2540 - Psalm 118:17

If the human mind is compared to a palace, the proper place for Christ's Word is on the throne!

Place for the Word,
Volume 44, Sermon #2584 - John 8:37

The proper place for the Word is inside, in your heart—have you got it hidden there?

Place for the Word,
Volume 44, Sermon #2584 - John 8:37

Oh, to have "the word of Christ" always dwelling inside of us;—in the memory, never forgotten; in the heart, always loved; in the understanding, really grasped; with all the powers and passions of the mind fully submitted to its control!

Christ's Indwelling Word,
Volume 46, Sermon #2679 - Colossians 3:16

I must honestly confess that before I knew the Lord, or was seriously seeking Him, although I found the historical parts of the Bible interesting, a great portion of the Scriptures appeared to me to be dull and meaningless.

Why Christ Is Not Esteemed,
Volume 53, Sermon #3033 - Isaiah 53:3

The main weapon which Christ wielded was "the Sword of the Spirit, which is the Word of God."

The Almighty Warrior,
Volume 58, Sermon #3292 - Psalm 45:3-5

If by reading the Scriptures we were only always reminded of the Holy Spirit. If we got no other good from the Scripture, itself, except the turning of our souls to think upon that Divine and blessed One, that would be, in itself, an inestimable blessing!

How to Read the Bible,
Volume 58, Sermon #3318 - 1 Timothy 4:13

There is a special curse pronounced upon any who shall add to this book; and you may rest assured that the Holy Spirit will not so transgress in a matter which he has peremptorily forbidden all his children to commit.

The Great Teacher and Remembrancer,
Volume 59, Sermon #3353 - John 14:26

Calling

In what way can I bring my Lord most glory, and be of most service to His Church while I am here? Solve that question, and pass into the practical.

An All Around Ministry, Page 233

If you think you can never honor Christ till you enter a pulpit, it may be just possible that you will afterwards honor him best by getting out of it as quickly as you can.

Saving Faith,
Volume 20, Sermon #1162 - Luke 7:50; Luke 18:42

It has come to be a dreadfully common belief in the Christian Church that the only man who has a "call" is the man who devotes all his time to what is called "the ministry," whereas all Christian service is ministry, and every Christian has a call to some kind of ministry or another.

A Golden Sentence,
Volume 55, Sermon #3135 - John 4:34

Calvinism

To me, Calvinism means the placing of the eternal God at the head of all things.

An All Around Ministry, Page 337

The doctrines of original sin, election, effectual calling, final perseverance, and all those great truths which are called Calvinism—though Calvin was not the author of them, but simply an able writer and preacher upon the subject—are, I believe, the essential doctrines of the Gospel that is in Jesus Christ. Now, I do not ask you whether you believe all this—it is possible you may not; but I believe you will before you enter heaven. I am persuaded, that as God may have washed your hearts, he will wash your brains before you enter heaven.

The Peculiar Sleep of the Beloved,
Volume 1, Sermon #12 - Psalm 127:2

Speaking of Arminians, Whitfield said, "We are all born Arminians." It is grace that turns us into Calvinists, grace that makes Christians of us, grace that makes us free, and makes us know our standing in Christ Jesus.

The Allegories of Sarah and Hagar,
Volume 2, Sermon #69 - Galatians 4:24

I hear one say, "Well, sir, you seem to be a fatalist!" No, far from it. There is just this difference between fate and providence. Fate is blind; providence has eyes. Fate is blind, a thing that must be; it is just an arrow shot from a bow, that must fly onward, but has no target. Not so, providence; providence is full of eyes. There is a design in everything, and an end to be answered; all things are working together, and working together for good.

Providence,
Volume 4, Sermon #187 - Matthew 10:30

Free will carried many a soul to hell, but never a soul to heaven.

Samson Conquered,
Volume 4, Sermon #224 - Judges 16:20, 21.

Your damnation is your own election, not God's; you richly deserve it.

Jacob and Esau,
Volume 5, Sermon #239 - Romans 9:13

That doctrine which is called "Calvinism" did not spring from Calvin; we believe that it sprang from the great founder of all truth.

Exposition of the Doctrines of Grace,
Volume 7, Sermon #385

Now, there are certain doctrines commonly called Calvinistic (but which ought never to have been called by such a name, for they are simply Christian doctrines) which I think commend themselves to the minds of all thoughtful persons, for this reason mainly, that they do ascribe to God everything.

Laus Deo, Volume 10,
Sermon #572 - Romans 11:36

I am not a Calvinist by choice, but because I cannot help it.

Dwell Deep, O Dedan,
Volume 18, Sermon #1085 - Jeremiah 49:8

You will find all true theology summed up in these two short sentences—salvation is all of the Grace of God—damnation is all of the will of man.

Why Some Seekers Are Not Saved,
Volume 41, Sermon #2411 - Isaiah. 59:1, 2

All who have heard the Gospel preached have been called to some extent. The Word of God calls every sinner to repent and trust the Savior, but that call brings nobody to Christ unless it is accompanied by the special effectual call of the Holy Spirit.

Speak, Lord!,
Volume 43, Sermon #2526 - 1 Samuel 3:10

I believe nothing merely because Calvin taught it, but because I have found his teaching in the Word of God.

Place for the Word,
Volume 44, Sermon #2584 - John 8:37

Some men cannot endure to hear the Doctrine of Election—I suppose they like to choose their own wives, but they are not willing that Christ should select His bride, the Church!

Hearing, Seeking, Finding,
Volume 44, Sermon #2590 - Psalm 132:6, 7

For it is not God's way to make men His servants, except so far as they willingly yield themselves to Him. He never violates the human will, though He constantly and effectually influences it.

Israel's Cry and God's Answer,
Volume 45, Sermon #2631 - Exodus 2:23-25; 3:9, 10

We do not come to Christ by the exertion of our own power to come, but by the cessation of the will to stay away!

The Old Gospel for the New Century,
Volume 47, Sermon #2708 - Matthew 11:28

Have you ever noticed, in the great summary of doctrines, that, as surely as you believe one, you must believe the rest? One doctrine so leans upon the others that, if you deny one, you must deny the rest. Some think that they can believe four out of the five points, and reject the last. It is impossible; God's truths are all joined together like links in a chain.

The Church of God and the Truth of God,
Volume 54, Sermon #3093 - 1 Timothy 3:15

We have in all our congregations a certain number of hearers who make great professions for a time, but afterwards go back and leave us. The reason very often being that the preaching has sifted them out from the wheat and proved that they are only chaff. I know that some of you feel very uncomfortable when I am preaching the Doctrine of Election or any of the other great Doctrines of Sovereign Grace. I am very sorry for any of you who cannot appreciate those glorious Truths of God in which my soul delights itself to the fullest—and I would earnestly and solemnly urge you to examine yourselves to see whether you have ever had Divine Grace in your hearts at all if you do not love to hear the Doctrines of Grace preached!

Clinging to Christ,
Volume 56, Sermon #3210 - John 6:67, 68.

They are all Calvinists there, every soul of them. They may have been Arminians on earth; thousands and millions of them were; but they are not after they get there, for here is their song, "Salvation unto our God, which sitteth upon the throne, and unto the Lamb."

The Multitude Before the Throne,
Volume 60, Sermon #3403 - Revelation 7:9, 10

Change

Alteration is not always improvement, as the pigeon said when she got out of the net and into the pie.

John Ploughman's Talk, Page 141

What's the use of traveling to the other end of the world to be worse off than you are?

John Ploughman's Talk, Page 160

Many a man has done exceedingly well in one sphere of life, but has not done so well in another sphere.

The Faithful Olive Tree,
Volume 56, Sermon #3208 - Judges 9:8, 9.

Character

Balance your duties, and let not one press out another.

Barbed Arrows, Page 21

A good name is better than a girdle of gold, and when that is gone, what has a man left?

John Ploughman's Pictures, Page 12

A godly character is the best tombstone.

John Ploughman's Talk, Page 170

Carve your name on hearts, and not on marble.

John Ploughman's Talk, Page 171

Our enemies cannot hurt us, unless we hurt ourselves. No man's character was ever really injured except by himself.

The World Turned Upside Down,
Volume 4, Sermon #193 - Acts 17:6

Bad men die out quickly, for the world feels it is a good thing to be rid of them; they are not worth remembering.

The Wicked Man's Life, Funeral and Epitaph,
Volume 4, Sermon #200 - Ecclesiastes 8:10

Truth lies between two extremes, and man, like a pendulum, swings either too much this way or that.

The Choice of a Leader,
Volume 21, Sermon #1248 - Luke 6:39, 40

You and I cannot be useful if we want to be sweet as honey in the mouths of men. God will never bless us if we wish to please men, that they may think well of us. Are you willing to tell them what will break your own heart in the telling and break theirs in the hearing? If not, you are not fit to serve the Lord. You must be willing to go and speak for God, though you will be rejected.

The Message from the Lord's Mouth,
Volume 24, Sermon #1431 - Ezekiel 3:17

The right way usually lies between two extremes: it is the narrow channel between the rock and the whirlpool.

Unprofitable Servants,
Volume 26, Sermon #1541 -
Matthew 25:30, Luke 17:10, Matthew 25:21

The reason why everything else loses its freshness to us is because of its want of variety.

The Dew of Christ's Youth,
Volume 47, Sermon #2724 - Psalm 110:3

Whatever is not divine, in due time must lose its freshness.

The Dew of Christ's Youth,
Volume 47, Sermon #2724 - Psalm 110:3

Perhaps our greatest weariness is weariness of ourselves. The one person that troubles me most is the one from whom I cannot get away as long as I am here.

Fourfold Satisfaction,
Volume 47, Sermon #2726 - Jeremiah 31:14, 25

Charismatic

When passion has run away with a man, who knows where it will carry him?

John Ploughman's Pictures, Page 143

Certain people are always on the look out for wonders and if they don't see them they invent them.

John Ploughman's Talk, Page 148

Some, I know, fall into a very vicious habit, which habit they excuse in themselves—namely, that of ordering their steps according to impressions. Every now and then I met with people whom I think to be rather weak in the head, who will journey from place to place, and will perform follies by the gross under the belief that they are doing the will of God, because some silly whim of their diseased brains is imagined to be an inspiration from above.

A Well-Ordered Life,
Volume 15, Sermon #878 - Psalm 119:133

Some religionists are deliriously happy, but they cannot tell you why. They can sing, and shout, and dance, but they can give no reason for their excitement. They see an enthusiastic crowd, and they catch the infection: their religion is purely emotional; I am not going to condemn it, yet show I unto you a more excellent way. The joy which is not created by substantial causes is mere froth and foam, and soon vanishes away. Unless you can tell why you are happy you will not long be happy.

The Tent Dissolved and the Mansion Entered,
Volume 29, Sermon #1719 - 2 Corinthians 5:1

The days of special visions, voices and prophesying have passed away, but we can still say with Peter, "We have a more sure word of prophecy; whereunto ye do well that ye take heed, as unto a light that shineth in a dark place, until the day dawn, and the day star arise in your hearts."

God's Hand at Evening,
Volume 58, Sermon #3290 - Ezekiel 33:22

Faith-healing is grand, but faith-enduring is grander.

Our Leader Through the Darkness,
Volume 59, Sermon #3370 - Isaiah 50:10, Isaiah 55:4

Seek not, therefore, after visions, fancies, miracles, signs, and wonders, but believe when God speaks to your heart, according to all the statutes and testimonies, the precepts and promises, which are contained in the sure word of revelation.

Assurance Sought,
Volume 63, Sermon #3546 - Psalm 35:3

Children

Habits soon become a second nature; to form new ones is hard work; but those formed in youth remain in old age.

Come Ye Children, Page 121

Now, to my mind, it seems that a father's experience is the best evidence that a young man can have of the truth of anything.

A Good Start, Page 46

That man is not worth hanging who does not love his mother.

John Ploughman's Pictures, Page 11

If young men knew the price of sin, even in this life, they would not be so hot to purchase pleasurable moments at the price of painful years.

Moab Is My Washpot,
Volume 17, Sermon #983 - Psalm 60:8

We also forget when we start in the battle of life that there is a great deal in novelty, and that novelty wears off.

Girding on the Harness,
Volume 20, Sermon #1193 - 1 Kings 20:11

Young people, you must pray, for your passions are strong, and your wisdom is little.

My Hourly Prayer,
Volume 28, Sermon #1657 - Psalm 119:117

Little children sometimes think they are wise, but they know nothing: wisdom is with their father, not with them.

On Humbling Ourselves Before God,
Volume 29, Sermon #1733 - 1 Peter 5:6

Young men, especially, are too apt to mistake the great enemy for a friend.

Young Man! A Prayer for You,
Volume 37, Sermon #2215 - 2 Kings 6:17

Christian Living

If any of you should ask me for an epitome of the Christian religion, I should say that it is in one word—prayer. Live and die without prayer, and you will pray long enough when you get to hell.

The Immutability of God,
Volume 1, Sermon #1 - Malachi 3:6

When you feel yourself to be utterly unworthy, you have hit the truth.

Unsound Spiritual Trading,
Volume 15, Sermon #849 - Proverbs 16:2

Faith works in us separateness from sinners.

Fearful of Coming Short,
Volume 20, Sermon #1177 - Hebrews 4:1, 2

A sheep in the midst of wolves is safe compared with the Christian in the midst of ungodly men.

Life's Need and Maintenance,
Volume 22, Sermon #1300 - Psalm 22:29

No life can surpass that of a man who quietly continues to serve God in the place where providence has placed him.

Enoch,
Volume 22, Sermon #1307 -
Genesis 5:21-24, Hebrews 11:5, 6, Jude 1:14, 15

If you are a child of God you are spoiled for the world.

Retreat Impossible,
Volume 23, Sermon #1341 - Judges 11:35

Man was made in the image of God, and nothing will satisfy man but God, in whose image he was made.

God Our Portion and His Word Our Treasure,
Volume 23, Sermon #1372 - Psalm 119:57

In our Lord's love we have the best motive for loyalty, the best reason for energy, and the best argument for perseverance.

Under Constraint,
Volume 24, Sermon #1411 - 2 Corinthians 5:14

We do not desire that our pattern should be lowered, but that our imitation should be raised.

A Heavenly Pattern for Our Earthly Life,
Volume 30, Sermon #1778 - Matthew 6:10

That religion which costs a man nothing is usually worth nothing.

The Threshing Floor of Ornan,
Volume 30, Sermon #1808 -
1 Chronicles 21:28, 1 Chronicles 22:1

Do you not know, dear friends, that the very essence of Christianity is for a man to deny himself?

All Or None - Or, Compromises Refused -
A Sermon with Five Texts, Volume 31,
Sermon #1830 - Exodus 10:26

Profess only what you possess, and rest only in that which has been given you from above.

The Form of Godliness Without the Power,
Volume 35, Sermon #2089 - 2 Timothy 3:5

All the works that we can ever do, be they what they may, can never bring such Glory to God as a single act of trust in Him!

No Fixity Without Faith,
Volume 39, Sermon #2305 - Isaiah 7:9

Charity and purity are the two garments of Christianity.

Charity and Purity,
Volume 39, Sermon #2313 - James 1:27

When you receive Christ into your heart, He cannot be taken away from you!

Take Eat,
Volume 40, Sermon #2350 - Matthew 26:26

Holiness is another name for salvation—to be delivered from the power of self-will, the domination of evil lusts and the tyranny of Satan—this is salvation.

the Rule and Reward of Serving Christ,
Volume 42, Sermon #2449 - John 12:26

The way to do a great deal is to keep on doing a little. The way to do nothing at all, is to be continually resolving that you will do everything.

Luminous Words,
Volume 43, Sermon #2549 - 1 Peter 4:1-3

A sense of satisfaction with yourself will be the death of your progress and it will prevent your sanctification.

God's Knowledge of Sin,
Volume 44, Sermon #2551 - Psalm 69:5

The more holy a man becomes, the more conscious he is of unholiness.

Waiting, Hoping, Watching,
Volume 44, Sermon #2579 - Psalm 130:5, 6

When a Christian man so lives that others see something about him which they do not perceive in themselves, that is one way in which they are often attracted towards the Christian life.

Ruth Deciding for God,
Volume 46, Sermon #2680 - Ruth 1:16

God always begins to work in a way that looks like undoing and not doing.

A Door of Hope,
Volume 47, Sermon #2750 - Hosea 2:15

One of the greatest rewards that we ever receive for serving God is the permission to do still more for Him.

David Warned and Rewarded,
Volume 48, Sermon #2775 - Psalm 19:11

"To glorify God and to enjoy Him forever" is the only worthy end of mortal man!

Barriers Obliterated,
Volume 49, Sermon #2847 - Isaiah 44:22

Do you not know that the higher you rise, even in the Church of Christ, the more responsibility you have, and the heavier burdens you have to carry?

Anxiety, Ambition, Indecision,
Volume 50, Sermon #2871 - Luke 12:29

If we were once to have a church fully awakened and zealous for Christ and His Truth, we should soon have the persecuting times back again.

"Who Is on the Lord's Side?"
Volume 50, Sermon #2884 - Exodus 32:26

Christ's kinship with His people is to be thought of with great comfort because it is voluntary.

Job's Sure Knowledge,
Volume 50, Sermon #2909 - Job 19:25

It is insulting to a man to call him a fool, but I question whether any man is saved unless he has called himself a fool!

An Old-Fashioned Remedy,
Volume 51, Sermon #2921 - Psalm 107:20

If we are, indeed, Christians, we have broken a great many idols, we have still some more to break and we must keep the hammer going till they are all broken!

Sham Conversion,
Volume 51, Sermon #2928 - 2 Kings 17:25, 33, 34

You worship not God at all if you do not worship God alone! There must be an image-breaking in the soul if the conversion is really true.

Sham Conversion,
Volume 51, Sermon #2928 - 2 Kings 17:25, 33, 34

Christians, you also are to love one another, not because of the gain which you get from one another, but rather because of the good you can do to one another.

Christ's "New Commandment",
Volume 51, Sermon #2936 - John 13:34, 35

"With God all things are possible," which means not only that God can do all things, but that we also can do all things when God is with us!

Unmitigated Prosperity,
Volume 51, Sermon #2963 - Isaiah 53:10

O Believer, whatever life of a spiritual kind you have in you, today, was given to you by God! It was not yours by nature.

His Great Love,
Volume 52, Sermon #2968 - Ephesians 2:4, 5

A way is none the less right because it is rough. Indeed, often it is all the more sure to be the right way because it is so displeasing to flesh and blood.

Angelic Protection in Appointed Ways,
Volume 52, Sermon #2969 - Psalm 91:11

A man never talks rightly of God's works till he knows God's ways. And it is idle to talk of them if there is no doing at the back of the talking.

Angelic Protection in Appointed Ways,
Volume 52, Sermon #2969 - Psalm 91:11

If ever you want to know what Christ means by His teaching, look at His life. You may rest assured that He never gave us a command which He was not, Himself, prepared to obey.

Thought Condemned, Yet Commanded,
Volume 52, Sermon #2973 - Matthew 6:31-33

As the planet needs the sun, so man needs his God. As the eye is nothing without light, so your spirit is nothing without God. You must have God!

The "Beau Ideal" of Life,
Volume 52, Sermon #2987 - Psalm 90:14

When a man plays the fool, let him do it for something that is worth having.

The "Beau Ideal" of Life,
Volume 52, Sermon #2987 - Psalm 90:14

Obedience to God is a flower that never grew on nature's dunghill! It grows only where the Spirit of God has tilled the soil and planted the root from which it springs.

An All-Important Question,
Volume 52, Sermon #3008 - John 9:35

Never dream that you can be pardoned and then be allowed to live as you did before—the very wish to do so would show that you were still under condemnation.

Good Cheer from Forgiven Sin,
Volume 52, Sermon #3016 - Matthew 9:2, Mark 2:3-5, Luke 5:18-20

If a man's prayer is of such a character that only sovereign Grace, real pardon and true salvation will content his soul, then he shall not be put off with anything else, but he shall have that for which his soul craves.

The Hungry Filled, the Rich Emptied,
Volume 52, Sermon #3019 - Luke 1:53

That man is truly happy who can say of all his substances, be it little or be it much, "the Lord gave it to me."

Fifteen Years After!,
Volume 53, Sermon #3025 - Job 1:21

Beloved, here is a test for us—is our religion a receiving religion, or is it a working and an earning religion? An earning religion sends souls to Hell. It is only a receiving religion that will take you to Heaven.

A Consistent Walk for Time to Come,
Volume 53, Sermon #3030 - Colossians 2:6

The true way for a Christian to live is to live entirely upon Christ.... Christians have experiences and they have feelings, but, if they are wise, they never feed upon these things, but upon Christ Himself.

A Consistent Walk for Time to Come,
Volume 53, Sermon #3030 - Colossians 2:6

A beggar with the Truth of God is mightier than priests and princes with a lie.

The Fashion of This World,
Volume 53, Sermon #3032 - 1 Corinthians 7:31

Sanctification is a lifelong work, continuously effected by the Holy Spirit, but justification is done in an instant! It is as complete the moment a sinner believes as when he stands before the Eternal! Is it not a marvelous thing that one moment should make you clean?

Pardon and Justification,
Volume 53, Sermon #3054 - Psalm 32:1

Nothing that man can present to God by way of sacrifice can ever purchase the blessing of forgiveness.

Pardon and Justification,
Volume 53, Sermon #3054 - Psalm 32:1

The way of sense is to get everything now—the way of faith is to get everything in God's time. The worldly man lives on the present—the Christian lives on the future.

An Observation of the Preacher,
Volume 53, Sermon #3072 - Ecclesiastes 7:8

Now, remember, you will never know the fulness of Christ until you know the emptiness of everything else but Christ.

Thrice Happy Day,
Volume 54, Sermon #3073 - Haggai 2:19

God has so made man's heart that nothing can ever fill it but God himself.

The Fourth Beatitude,
Volume 55, Sermon #3157 - Matthew 5:6

We need, nowadays, dear Friends, to have a little less talk about what men are and much more actual living unto Jesus. The Lord work it in us by His Spirit!

Concentration and Diffusion,
Volume 55, Sermon #3174 - John 12:3

Surely the Lord does not create life in the regenerated soul without providing stores upon which it may be nourished! Where He gives life, He gives food.

How the Lambs Feed,
Volume 56, Sermon #3199 - Isaiah 5:17

Do you think God would make us so dissatisfied with this world if he did not mean to satisfy us with another and a better one?

Strangers and Sojourners,
Volume 57, Sermon #3234 - Psalm 39:12

If grace does not make you to differ from your own surroundings, is it really grace at all?

Confession of Christ,
Volume 60, Sermon #3405 - Matthew 10:32, 33

The Church

A church is a soul-saving company or it is nothing.

The Greatest Fight in the World, Page 46

The elect church is saved that she may save, cleansed that she may cleanse, blessed that she may bless.

The Greatest Fight in the World, Page 48

The elect church is the favorite of heaven, the treasure of Christ, the crown of His head, the bracelet of His arm, the breastplate of His heart, the very centre and core of His love.

Morning and Evening, Page 161

To introduce unconverted persons to the church is to weaken and degrade it; and therefore an apparent gain may be a real loss.

The Soul Winner, Page 13

In proportion as a church is holy, in that proportion will its testimony for Christ be powerful.

Words of Counsel, Page 71

The eyes of the world are intended to be checks upon the church.

The Tabernacle-Outside the Camp,
Volume 7, Sermon #359 - Exodus 33:7

Divisions in Churches never begin with those full of love to the Savior.

True Unity Promoted,
Volume 11, Sermon #607 - Ephesians 4:3

An unwatchful church will soon become an unholy church.

Sleep Not,
Volume 17, Sermon #1022 - 1 Thessalonians 5:6

The new converts put fresh blood into the veins of the church.

A Holy Celebration,
Volume 19, Sermon #1092 - Exodus 12:42

God will not cause his children to be born where there are none to nurse them; he will be sure not to send converts to churches which do not want them.

Additions to the Church,
Volume 20, Sermon #1167 - Acts 2:47

I have observed that churches which do not care for the outlying population speedily suffer from disunion and strife.

"By All Means, Save Some",
Volume 20, Sermon #1170 - 1 Corinthians 9:22

The church is not perfect, but woe to the man who finds pleasure in pointing out her imperfections. Christ loved his church, and let us do the same. I have no doubt that the Lord can see more fault in his church than I can; and I have equal confidence that he sees no fault at all. Because he covers her faults with his own love—that love which covers a multitude of sins; and he removes all her defilement with that precious blood which washes away all the transgressions of his people.

"By All Means, Save Some",
Volume 20, Sermon #1170 - 1 Corinthians 9:22

Fighting sheep are strange animals, and fighting Christians are self-evident contradictions.

Sheep Among Wolves,
Volume 23, Sermon #1370 - Matthew 10:16

I think any minister will tell you it is the people who do nothing themselves in a church that find fault with those who do the work.

With the King for His Work!,
Volume 24, Sermon #1400 - 1 Chronicles 4:23

The church would be one with itself if it were one with the truth.

The Message from the Lord's Mouth,
Volume 24, Sermon #1431 - Ezekiel 3:17

The church needs young blood in its veins. Our strength for holding the faith may lie in experienced saints but our zeal for propagating it must be found in the young.

Others to Be Granted In,
Volume 24, Sermon #1437 - Isaiah 56:8

Late attendance frequently means heartless worship, disturbance, and distraction.

The Mediator—Judge and Savior,
Volume 26, Sermon #1540 - Acts 10:42, 43

I never heard of quarrels among devils, nor did I ever read of sects in hell: they are all one in their hatred of the Christ and of God.

Our Lord's Trial Before the Sanhedrin,
Volume 28, Sermon #1643 - Mark 14:64

A church may have a very short muster-roll, and yet it may be very dear to God, who thinks more of quality than of quantity, more of obedience than of numbers.

Commendation for the Steadfast,
Volume 30, Sermon #1814 - Revelation 3:8, 10

As a church we must love Jesus, or else we have lost our reason for existence.

Love's Complaining,
Volume 32, Sermon #1926 - Revelation 2:4, 5

As a rule, I believe congregations get out of a minister what they put into him; that is to say, if they pray much for him, God will give him much blessing for them.

The Filling of Empty Vessels,
Volume 35, Sermon #2063 - 2 Kings 4:3

To be driven from church to church, as some are, is a wretched business. To be like others, changing their views as often as the moon; happy nowhere, miserable everywhere, agreeing with nobody, not even with themselves, is a poor business.

Essential Points in Prayer,
Volume 35, Sermon #2064 - 1 Kings 9:2, 3

Beloved, if it had been possible to destroy the church of God on earth, it would have been destroyed long ago.

Our Expectation,
Volume 37, Sermon #2186 - Isaiah 53:10

Half the strength of the church goes in ambulance service towards the weak and wounded.

The Census of Israel,
Volume 37, Sermon #2198 - Numbers 16:66

Where would have been our flourishing churches of today if our forefathers had disdained to sustain them while they were yet in their infancy?

Small Things Not to Be Despised,
Volume 44, Sermon #2601 - Zechariah 4:10

There is always a set of grumblers about who think they could preach better and manage Sunday schools better than anybody else. They are the people who generally do nothing at all.

Christ's Love for His Vineyard,
Volume 48, Sermon #2785 - Song of Solomon 8:12

Stagnation in a church is the devil's delight.

Lukewarmness,
Volume 48, Sermon #2802 - Revelation 3:15, 16

The most powerful enemy of the Church can do nothing without God's permission!

An Instructive Truth,
Volume 50, Sermon #2893 - Jeremiah 10:23

I would recommend you to choose the church of which you would be a member and the pastor whom you would hear by this one thing—by how much of Christ there is in that church and how much of the savor of Christ there is in that ministry!

A Sermon from a Sick Preacher,
Volume 52, Sermon #3014 - 1 Peter 2:7

God will honor His Church when she has faith enough to believe in His promises.

"And It Was So",
Volume 53, Sermon #3064 - Genesis 1:7

Whatever may happen to denominations, whatever divisions we may live to see, let it still be known that for God and His Truth we are prepared to hold our ground at any expense or at any risk.

The Church of God and the Truth of God,
Volume 54, Sermon #3093 - 1 Timothy 3:15

The church nowadays is for the most part too strong, too wise, too self-dependent, to do much.

The Great Pot and the Twenty Loaves,
Volume 56, Sermon #3187 - 2 Kings 4:38, 41, 42

Any hypocrite comes on a Sunday, but they do not, to my knowledge, all of them come on Monday to the prayer-meeting, nor all to the week-night service on a Thursday. I am pretty certain of this, though some of them may. Week-night meetings and services are a powerful test.

Joining the Church,
Volume 60, Sermon #3411 - 2 Corinthians 8:5

Comfort

Within the Scripture there is a balm for every wound, a salve for every sore.

The Greatest Fight in the World, Page 15

Did you ever notice how the Bible ends? It closes with that happiest of conclusions, marriage and happiness.

Prospect - "He Will Keep,"
Volume 32, Sermon #1883 - John 17:11, 12

Surely there is no greater comfort under Heaven than a sense of sin forgiven and of reconciliation to God by the death of His Son!

The Secret of Happiness,
Volume 56, Sermon #3227 - Matthew 9:2

Compassion

An escape from suffering would be an escape from the power to sympathize, and that were to be deprecated beyond all things.

For the Troubled,
Volume 19, Sermon #1090 - Psalm 88:7

Look at sinful men as mad, and you will pity them and bear with them.

Compassion on the Ignorant,
Volume 24, Sermon #1407 - Hebrews 5:2

I do not know how else we could care for some poor creatures, if it were not that Jesus teaches us to despise none and despair of none.

Under Constraint,
Volume 24, Sermon #1411 - 2 Corinthians 5:14

A Jesus who never wept could never wipe away my tears.

"Jesus Wept,"
Volume 35, Sermon #2091 - John 11:35

Compromise

To pursue union at the expense of truth is treason to the Lord Jesus.

The Down Grade Controversy, Page 34

Better die than sell your soul to the highest bidder.

John Ploughman's Pictures, Page 122

There is a time to do as others wish, and a time to refuse.

John Ploughman's Talk, Page 32

But we are so gentle and quiet, we do not use strong language about other people's opinions; but let men go to hell out of charity to them.

Words of Counsel, Page 33

Do you not know that a person who is silent when a wrong thing is said or done may become a participator in the sin?

Words of Wisdom, Page 148

Be more concerned to be right than to be happy.

"The Time of Jacob's Trouble,"
Volume 45, Sermon #2645 - Jeremiah 30:7

If you love Christ but little, you will hate error but little. If you do not love the truth at all, you will not hate error at all.

Love and Jealousy,
Volume 62, Sermon #3516 - Song of Solomon 8:6

Conversation

Every time the sheep bleats, it loses a mouthful, and every time we complain we lose a blessing.

John Ploughman's Talk, Page 43

How much of the staple of our conversation consists in complaint!

The Overflowing Cup,
Volume 15, Sermon #874 - Psalm 23:5

Creation

For our part, we find it far more easy to believe that the Lord made us than that we were developed by a long chain of natural selections from floating atoms which fashioned themselves.

The Treasury of David,
Psalms 100, Verse 3

The design argument, when brought to bear upon nature, proves the existence of God. We see in nature clear marks of design, and a design argues a designer.

The Whole-Heartedness of God in Blessing His People,
Volume 34, Sermon #2036 - Jeremiah 32:41

Men fail to see the miracle which God is working in every living thing.

Reasons for Seeking God,
Volume 53, Sermon #3034 - Amos 5:8

Culture

Time impairs all things, the fashion becomes obsolete and passes away.

The Treasury of David,
Psalms 102, Verse 26

If any man love the world the love of the Father is not in him, and he who has the smile of the ungodly must look for the frown of God.

Counting the Cost,
Volume 20, Sermon #1159 - Luke 14:28-30

How many of you look around on society to know what to do; you watch the general current, and then float upon it; you study the popular breeze and shift your sails to suit it. True men do not so. You ask—Is it fashionable? If it be fashionable, it must be done. Fashion is the law of multitudes, but it is nothing more than the common consent of fools. The world has its fashions in religion as well as in dress, and many of you feel the influence of it.

Decision-Illustrated by the Case of Joshua,
Volume 21, Sermon #1229 - Joshua 24:15

To be abreast of the times is to be an enemy of God.

A Luther Sermon at the Tabernacle,
Volume 29, Sermon #1749 - Habakkuk 2:4

I am always glad when men cannot be happy in the world; for, as long as they can be, they will be.

How God Comes to Man,
Volume 50, Sermon #2900 - Genesis 3:8, 9

Any kind of fashion, which may rule the hour, draws a mad crowd after it. No matter how absurd or ridiculous the mania, the worshippers of fashion cry, "These be thy gods, O Israel." Yes, Satan is marvelously well obeyed by his servants.

Landlord and Tenant,
Volume 53, Sermon #3021 - Isaiah 38:1

It is a world of toil, and I believe that it will go on so; and instead of getting better, the world will in some respects get worse.

A World Wide Welcome,
Volume 59, Sermon #3352 - Matthew 11:28

God has not made this world to be a nest for us, and if we try to make it such for ourselves, he plants thorns in it, so that we may be compelled to mount and find our soul's true home somewhere else, in a higher and nobler sphere than this poor world can give.

Fearing and Trusting—Trusting and Not Fearing,
Volume 59, Sermon #3362 - Psalm 56:3, Isaiah 12:2

Death

May we regard death as the most weighty of all events, and be sobered by its approach.

Morning and Evening, Page 541

He who does not prepare for death is more than an ordinary fool, he is a madman.

Morning and Evening, Page 541

How well should those live who are to live so little!

The Treasury of David,
Psalms 39, Verse 5

Here is the history of the grass—sown, grown, blown, mown, gone; and the history of man is not much more.

The Treasury of David, Psalms 90, Verse 6

Now, I believe the sight of a funeral is a very healthful thing for the soul.

The Wicked Man's Life, Funeral and Epitaph,
Volume 4, Sermon #200 - Ecclesiastes 8:10

You and I hear of sudden deaths, and yet we imagine we shall not die suddenly.

An Earnest Invitation,
Volume 5, Sermon #260 - Psalm 2:12

The young may die: the old must.

A Song, a Solace, a Sermon and a Summons,
Volume 13, Sermon #787 - Psalm 136:1

Men have usually shown us what lies at the bottom of their heart when they have come to die.

The Last Lookout,
Volume 17, Sermon #989 - 2 Timothy 4:6

We wept when we were born though all around us smiled; so shall we smile when we die while all around us weep.

Stephen's Death,
Volume 20, Sermon #1175 - Acts 7:59, 60

We have heard of one who, when the morning paper brought him news that a friend in business had died, was drawing on his boots to go to his counting-house, and observed with a laugh that as far as he was concerned, he was so busy he had no time to die. Yet, ere the words were finished, he fell forward and was a corpse.

Christ the Destroyer of Death,
Volume 22, Sermon #1329 - 1 Corinthians 15:26

St. Augustine used to say he did not know whether to call it a dying life or a living death, and I leave you the choice between those two expressions. This is certainly a dying life; its march is marked by graves. Nothing but a continuous miracle keeps any one of us from the sepulchre. Were omnipotence to stay its power but for a moment, earth would return to earth, and ashes to ashes. It is a dying life: and equally true is it that it is a living death. We are always dying. Every beating pulse we tell leaves but the number less: the more years we count in our life, the fewer remain in which we shall behold the light of day.

What Is Your Life?,
Volume 30, Sermon #1773 - James 4:14

We are all moving, and yet we do not perceive it; even so while you are listening to this sermon you are all being borne onward towards eternity at lightning speed.

What Is Your Life?,
Volume 30, Sermon #1773 - James 4:14

Dying does not mean ceasing to exist, for Adam did not cease to exist, nor do those who die.

Death and Life,
Volume 31, Sermon #1868 - Romans 6:23

Yesterday I was born: to-day I live: tomorrow I must die.

But a Step,
Volume 31, Sermon #1870 - 1 Samuel 20:3

Death is no punishment to the believer: it is the gate of endless joy.

Healing and Pardon,
Volume 32, Sermon #1905 - Isaiah 33:24

Where death finds you eternity will leave you.

Eternal Life Within Present Grasp,
Volume 33, Sermon #1946 - 1 Timothy 6:12,19

The Lord will give dying grace in dying moments.

Crossing the Jordan,
Volume 34, Sermon #2039 - Joshua 1:10, 11

Nothing upon earth ever gives me so much establishment in the faith as to visit members of this church when they are about to die.

The Bible Tried and Proved,
Volume 35, Sermon #2084 - Psalm 12:6

We feel a thousand deaths in fearing one.

Sowing in the Wind, Reaping Under Clouds,
Volume 38, Sermon #2264 - Ecclesiastes 11:4

Are you afraid of dying? Oh! never be afraid of that; be afraid of living. Living is the only thing which can do any mischief; dying never can hurt a Christian.

The Dumb Singing,
Volume 45, Sermon #2625 - Isaiah 35:5

Oh, if we could not die, it would be indeed horrible! Who wants to be chained to this poor life for a century or longer?

Fallen Asleep,
Volume 46, Sermon #2659 - 1 Corinthians 15:6

It is a very natural thing that man should fear to die, for man was not originally created to die.

The Fear of Death,
Volume 55, Sermon #3125 - Hebrews 2:15

The Christian who contemplates death with joy is a living sermon.

The Fear of Death,
Volume 55, Sermon #3125 - Hebrews 2:15

My observation warrants me in remarking that the most of Christians, when they die, are either in a deep calm or else triumphant in an ecstasy of delight.

The Fear of Death,
Volume 58, Sermon #3286 - Hebrews 2:14, 15

You are nearer home than you thought you were, and every moment you are getting nearer still.

Life's Inevitable Burden,
Volume 59, Sermon #3355 - Galatians 6:6

Depravity

The Lord knows very well that you cannot change your own heart and cannot cleanse your own nature, but He also knows that He can do both.

All of Grace, Page 36

In the best prayer that was ever offered by the holiest man that ever lived, there was enough of sin to render it a polluted thing if the Lord had looked upon it by itself.

Golden Bowls Full of Incense,
Volume 18, Sermon #1051 - Revelation 5:8

A very hell of corruption lies within the best saint; and if the grace of God did not restrain it, he would soon be found among the chief of sinners.

Acceptable Service,
Volume 28, Sermon #1639 - Hebrews 12:28, 29

The cross rejected is the clearest proof of the heart depraved.

The Wedding Was Furnished with Guests,
Volume 34, Sermon #2022 - Matthew 22:10

If any man could see his own heart as it is by nature, he would be driven mad: the sight of our disease is not to be borne unless we also see the remedy.

The Mediator-the Interpreter,
Volume 35, Sermon #2097 - Exodus 20:18-20

No man's reason would survive a full sight of his own inner self.

The Rough Hewer,
Volume 36, Sermon #2134 - Hosea 6:4, 5

Even concerning those who have heard the Gospel, it can still be said, "They have not all obeyed the Gospel." and this, dear Friends, is one of the plainest proofs of the deep depravity of human nature.

Disobedience to the Gospel,
Volume 48, Sermon #2804 - Romans 10:16

The creature that has done nothing right, but everything that is wrong, still believes in himself.

No Fixity Without Faith,
Volume 39, Sermon #2305 - Isaiah 7:9

No, sir, you are even worse in heart than you ever were in life, because there are many things that restrain you from revealing your naked self to those who only see your outward life.

False Justification and True,
Volume 51, Sermon #2932 - Job 9:20, Romans 8:33, 34

O Believer, whatever life of a spiritual kind you have in you, today, was given to you by God! It was not yours by nature.

His Great Love,
Volume 52, Sermon #2968 - Ephesians 2:4, 5

We say it sincerely, for we know how sadly true it is—the natural heart of man never does and never can produce so much as one single grain that God can receive as being to His honor and glory.

The Vision of the Field,
Volume 52, Sermon #3001 - Ezekiel 36:9

It is an astounding thing and a great proof of human depravity that men do not themselves seek salvation. They even deny the necessity of it and would sooner run away than be partakers of it!

The Errand of Mercy,
Volume 53, Sermon #3050 - Luke 19:10

Men go astray from God by nature, but they only return to God through Grace.

Christ's Ambassadors,
Volume 55, Sermon #3148 - 2 Corinthians 5:20

Here is His handiwork all around us, most fair and beautiful, yet the fool says in his heart, "There is no God," and proves himself to be a fool by saying it!

Strangers and Sojourners,
Volume 57, Sermon #3234 - Psalm 39:12

Fallen man, whether he knows it or not, is spiritually a beggar.

Beggars Becoming Princes,
Volume 57, Sermon #3256 - 1 Samuel 2:8

Depression

To have something to do for Jesus, and to go right on with it, is one of the best ways to get over a bereavement, or any heavy mental depression. If you can pursue some great object, you will not feel that you are living for nothing.

We Endeavor, Page 81

Better to have a Christian's days of sorrow, than a worldling's days of mirth.

Words of Cheer, Page 87

Depression of spirit often leads to slackness of hand.

Divine Love and Its Gifts,
Volume 19, Sermon #1096 - 2 Thessalonians 2:16, 17

The worst forms of depression are cured when Holy Scripture is believed.

The Bible Tried and Proved,
Volume 35, Sermon #2084 - Psalm 12:6

The condition of our Grace does not always coincide with the state of our joys. We may be rich in faith and love, and yet have so low an esteem of ourselves as to be much depressed.

Over the Mountains,
Volume 58, Sermon #3307 - Solomon's Song 2:16, 17

You cannot always rejoice, because, although your treasure is not in this world, your affliction is.

Fullness of Joy Our Privilege,
Volume 60, Sermon #3406 - 1 John 1:4

It is a good thing for the melancholy to become a Christian; it is an unfortunate thing for the Christian to become melancholy.

Joy In Salvation,
Volume 62, Sermon #3503 - Psalm 9:4

Desires

You may judge a man by what he groans after.

Morning and Evening, Page 679

It cannot be that my Lord has made me sick of this world, and yet will not give me another.

Partnership with Christ,
Volume 44, Sermon #2580 - 1 Corinthians 1:9

Do not think first of the desires of your heart, but think first of delighting yourself in your God! If you have accepted Him as your Lord, He is yours, so delight in Him and then He will give you the desires of your heart.

Facts and Inferences,
Volume 57, Sermon #3232 - Psalm 37:35-37

Why, the Christian, above all men, should have what the world calls his, "holidays and bonfire nights"—his days of rejoicing, times of holy laughter, seasons of overflowing delight. No, I think he should strive to have them always, for we are told, "Delight yourself in the Lord, and He shall give you the desires of your heart!"

The Truly Blessed Man,
Volume 57, Sermon #3270 - Psalm 1:1-3

Devil

When I hear a Christian man finding fault with his minister, I always wish that the devil had found somebody else to do his dirty work.

Christ's "New Commandment",
Volume 51, Sermon #2936 - John 13:34, 35

Discipleship

He cannot be a disciple who does not learn, but invents.

The Child of Light Walking in Light,
Volume 33, Sermon #1986 - 1 John 1:6, 7

You cannot be Christ's servant if you are not willing to follow him, cross and all. What do you crave? A crown? Then it must be a crown of thorns if you are to be like him. Do you want to be lifted up? So you shall, but it will be upon a cross.

Precepts and Promises,
Volume 50, Sermon #2874 - John 12:26

God in his providence and in grace, as far as we have been made willing to learn of him, is educating us for something higher than this world.

The Divine Discipline,
Volume 59, Sermon #3335 - Deuteronomy 32:11, 12

Doctrine

The path of truth in doctrine is generally a middle one.

Words of Counsel, Page 35

Men go after novel and false doctrines because they do not really know the truth; for if the truth had gotten into them and filled them, they would not have room for these day-dreams.

A Good Start, Page 108

Whether you are Calvinists, or Arminians, or anything else, dear friends, be first and chiefly Christians—Christians—following Christ, receiving him as the great Expositor to you of God, and of the great truths of revelation. You will tell me you have your "bodies of divinity;" there never was but one "body of divinity," and that was the "body" of the man, Christ Jesus; do you, abating all prejudices and self-formed opinions, receive our Lord as the great embodiment of truth.

Open Heart for the Great Savior,
Volume 12, Sermon #669 - John 1:12

Orthodoxy is my doxy; heterodoxy is anybody else's doxy who does not agree with me.

Lessons from Nature,
Volume 17, Sermon #1005 - Psalm 104:17, 18

All systems of theology, except that which is founded upon free grace, in some way or other take off the edge of guilt.

The Faithful Saying,
Volume 24, Sermon #1416 - 1 Timothy 1:15

The theology of the present aims at the deification of man, but the truth of all time magnifies God.

Faith Essential to Pleasing God,
Volume 35, Sermon #2100 - Hebrews 11:6

Dry doctrine, without the damping of the Spirit of God, may only make fuel for your eternal destruction.

Clear Shining After Rain,
Volume 38, Sermon #2284 - 2 Samuel 23:4

This is the doctrine that we preach; if a man be saved, all the honor is to be given to Christ; but if a man be lost, all the blame is to be laid upon himself. You will find all true theology summed up in these two short sentences, salvation is all of the grace of God, damnation is all of the will of man.

Why Some Seekers Are Not Saved,
Volume 41, Sermon #2411 - Isaiah. 59:1, 2

If you meet with a system of theology which magnifies man, flee from it as far as you can.

"Non, Nobis Domine!",
Volume 48. Sermon #2784 - Psalm 115:1

The teachers of the modern school of theology work in a kind of god-factory.

Conceit Rebuked,
Volume 49, Sermon #2834 - Job 34:33

"Then," say some, "tell us how to discern the truth." You may judge of it by three things; by God, by Christ, and by man; that is, the truth which honors God, the truth which glorifies Christ, and the truth which humbles man.

The Church of God and the Truth of God,
Volume 54, Sermon #3093 - 1 Timothy 3:15

All errors will die in due time.

Established Work,
Volume 55, Sermon #3142 - Psalm 90:17

Doubt

Our failure lies in want of faith, not in excess of it. It would be hard to believe God too much: it is dreadfully common to believe him too little.

According to Promise, Page 89

We believe on evidence. Now the most foolish part of many men's doubts, is, that they do not doubt on evidence.

Mr. Fearing Comforted,
Volume 5, Sermon #246 - Matthew 14:31

Atheism denies God's existence—unbelief denies his goodness, and since goodness is essential to God, these doubts do, in reality, stab at his very being.

The Danger of Doubting,
Volume 8, Sermon #439 - 1 Samuel 27:1

Would it not be better to be dumb when we are doubtful? Muzzle that dog of unbelief!

Gratitude for Deliverance From the Grave,
Volume 38, Sermon #2237 - Psalm 118:17, 18

I usually find that the greatest doubters are the people who do not read the Bible.

How Faith Comes,
Volume 45, Sermon #2623 - John 4:39-42

Doubt thee, my Lord? I could doubt all except thee; and doubt myself most of all.

Faith Without Sight,
Volume 47, Sermon #2721 - John 20:29

Education

The best education is education in the best things.

The Treasury of David,
Psalms 78, Verse 4

Do not think Christians are made by education; they are made by creation.

Light-Natural and Spiritual,
Volume 11, Sermon #660 - Genesis 1:1-5.

Election

If God has set his choice upon us, let us aim to be choice men.

The Treasury of David,
Psalms 105, Verse 6

Many persons want to know their election before they look to Christ, but they cannot learn it thus, it is only to be discovered by "looking unto Jesus."

Morning and Evening, Page 398

Electing love has selected some of the worst to be made the best.

Morning and Evening, Page 684

I believe the doctrine of election, because I am quite sure that if God had not chosen me I should never have chosen him; and I am sure he chose me before I was born, or else he never would have chosen me afterwards; and he must have elected me for reasons unknown to me, for I never could find any reason in myself why he should have looked upon me with special love.

Lectures to My Students,
Volume 2, Page 47

Your damnation is your own election, not God's; you richly deserve it.

Jacob and Esau,
Volume 5, Sermon #239 - Romans 9:13

Our Arminian antagonists always leave the fallen angels out of the question: for it is not convenient to them to recollect this ancient instance of Election. They call it unjust, that God should choose one man and not another. By what reasoning can this be unjust when they will admit that it was righteous enough in God to choose one race—the race of men, and leave another race—the race of angels, to be sunk into misery on account of sin.

Election and Holiness,
Volume 6, Sermon #303 - Deuteronomy 10:14-16

Grace does not choose a man and leave him as he is.

The Woman Which Was a Sinner,
Volume 14, Sermon #801 - Luke 7:37-38

The Lord knows how, without violating the human will (which he never does), so to influence the heart that the man with full consent, against his former will, yields to the will of God, and is made willing in the day of God's power.

Amazing Grace,
Volume 22, Sermon #1279 - Isaiah 57:18

We see our election by our calling, and not else.

Why May I Rejoice?,
Volume 22, Sermon #1321 - Luke 10:20

There is no man in this world chosen to go to heaven apart from being made fit to go there.

Refined, But Not with Silver,
Volume 24, Sermon #1430 - Isaiah 48:10

Foreordination to holiness is indissolubly joined to foreordination to happiness.

The Singular Origin of a Christian,
Volume 31, Sermon #1829 - Ephesians 2:10

God's choice of us was not because we were holy, but to make us holy; and God's purpose will not be fulfilled unless we are made holy.

Blessing for Blessing,
Volume 38, Sermon #2266 - Ephesians 1:3, 4

I believe that God will save his own elect, and I also believe that, if I do not preach the gospel, the blood of men will be laid at my door.

Three Arrows-Or Six?,
Volume 39, Sermon #2303 - 2 Kings 13:18, 19

Whatever may be said about the doctrine of election, it is written in the Word of God as with an iron pen, and there is no getting rid of it; there it stands.

The Beloved Pastor's Plea for Unity,
Volume 39, Sermon #2320 - Romans 1:7

To this day, men cannot bear that doctrine. Free will suits them very well, but free grace does not. They would not let Christ choose his own wife; I say it with the utmost reverence.

Must He?,
Volume 47, Sermon #2755 - Luke 19:5

The way for you to ascertain God's choice is to talk about Christ to everybody you meet; try to bring everyone to Christ. The Lord will do the sorting far better than you can; he never makes a mistake.

Heart-Communing,
Volume 48, Sermon #2779 - 1 Kings 10:2

God does not save an unwilling man, but he makes him willing in the day of his power.

New Tokens on Ancient Love,
Volume 50, Sermon #2880 - Jeremiah 31:3

You cannot see God till your heart is changed, till your nature is renewed, till your actions, in the tenor of them, shall become such as God would have them to be.

Holiness Demanded,
Volume 50, Sermon #2902 - Hebrews 12:14

Some people seem to be afraid lest we should be the means of saving some of the non-elect—but that is a fear which never troubles either my head or my heart, for I know that with all the effort and preaching in the world, we shall never bring more to Christ than Christ has had given to Him by His Father!

Too Little for the Lamb,
Volume 51, Sermon #2937 - Exodus 12:3, 4

The Lord, then, has a people whom He regards with a special love which is not shed abroad in the hearts of others. These people He set apart for Himself from eternity.

God Comforting His People,
Volume 52, Sermon #3012 - Isaiah 49:13

Stagger not at electing love; it is one of the highest notes of heavenly music.

The Spirits office Towards Disciples,
Volume 53, Sermon #3062 - John 16:14

Now, you need not ask tonight whether you are God's elect. I ask another question—Do you believe on the Lord Jesus Christ? If you do, you are His elect—if you do not, the question is not to be decided by us yet. If you are God's chosen ones, you will know it by your trusting in Jesus. Simple as that trust is, it is the Infallible proof of election! God never sets the brand of faith upon a soul whom Christ had not bought with His blood. And if you believe, all eternity is yours! Your name is in God's Book, you are a favored one of Heaven, the Divine decrees all point to you—go your way and rejoice!

The True Aim of Preaching,
Volume 56, Sermon #3191 - Acts 13:38

If you are God's chosen ones, you will know it by your trusting in Jesus. Simple as that trust is, it is the infallible proof of election.

The True Aim of Preaching,
Volume 56, Sermon #3191 - Acts 13:38

It is an inspiration for us all to work for Christ, because we are sure to have some results.

The Wondrous Covenant,
Volume 58, Sermon #3326 - Hebrews 8:10

They who seek Christ are already being sought of him.

Knowing and Believing,
Volume 58, Sermon #3331 - 2 Timothy 1:12

Long before time had begun, God had foreknown his chosen, and foreordained them unto eternal life. They had not chosen him, for they were not in existence.

God's Mercy Going Before,
Volume 60, Sermon #3413 - Psalm 59:10

In one sense, no man comes to God with compulsion; and in another sense, no man comes without compulsion.

The Desire of All Nations,
Volume 61, Sermon #3442 - Haggai 2:7

Emotions

Judged by changeful feelings, one might be lost and saved a dozen times a day.

Consolation for the Despairing,
Volume 19, Sermon #1146 - Psalm 31:22

That which is wrought by noise will subside when quiet reigns, as the bubble dies with the wave which bore it.

The Gentleness of Jesus,
Volume 19, Sermon #1147 - Matthew 12:19, 20, 21

The value of feeling depends upon its cause.

Our Leader Through the Darkness,
Volume 59, Sermon #3370 - Isaiah 50:10, Isaiah 55:4

Entertainment

"But," says one, "are we not to have amusements?" Yes, such amusements as you can take in the fear of God. Do whatever Jesus would have done.

A Good Start, Page 291

Eschatology

It is only Christ's coming that can make a millennium.

Perfect Cleansing,
Volume 7, Sermon #379 - Joel 3:21

I do not think we should be so certain of death as some Christians are, because the Lord's coming is much more certain than our dying.

Death and Life in Christ,
Volume 9, Sermon #503 - Romans 6:8-11

Some think that this descent of the Lord will be post-millennial—that is, after the thousand years of his reign. I cannot think so. I conceive that the advent will be pre-millennial; that he will come first; and then will come the millennium as the result of his personal reign upon earth.

Justification and Glory,
Volume 11, Sermon #627 - Romans 8:30

Some hearers are crazy after the mysteries of the future. Well, there are two or three brethren in London who are always trumpeting and vialing. Go and hear them if you want it, I have something else to do.

Rightly Dividing the Word of Truth,
Volume 21, Sermon #1217 - 2 Timothy 2:15

The Lord's "quickly" may not be my "quickly"; and if so, let him do what seems good to him!

The Two "Comes,"
Volume 23, Sermon #1331 - Revelation 22:17

If his first coming does not give you eternal life, his second coming will not. If you do not hide in his wounds when he comes as your Savior, there will be no hiding place for you when he comes as your Judge.

"He Comes with Clouds,"
Volume 33, Sermon #1989 - Revelation 1:7

I think that the millennium will commence after his coming, and not before it. I cannot imagine the kingdom with the King absent.

Watching for Christ's Coming,
Volume 39, Sermon #2302 - Luke 12:37, 38

Notice, next, dear friends, that it is not good for you to know the times and the seasons. That is what the savior means when he says, "It is not for you to know." for, first, it would distract your attention from the great things of which you have to think.

Witnessing Better Than Knowing the Future,
Volume 39, Sermon #2330 - Acts 1:6-8

We may make our prophetic charts if we like, but God will follow his own chart.

The Lord's Knowledge, Our Safeguard,
Volume 41, Sermon #2441 - 2 Peter 2:9

Eternity

A seat in heaven shall one day be mine; but a chain in hell would have been mine if grace had not changed me.

The Fruitless Vine,
Volume 3, Sermon #125 - Ezekiel 15:1, 2

If sinners be damned, at least let them leap to Hell over our dead bodies. And if they perish, let them perish with our arms wrapped about their knees, imploring them to stay. If Hell must be filled, let it be filled in the teeth of our exertions, and let not one go unwarned and unprayed for.

The Wailing of Risca,
Volume 7, Sermon #349 - Jeremiah 4:20

Better to go to heaven alone than to hell with a herd.

A Well-Ordered Life,
Volume 15, Sermon #878 - Psalm 119:133

While you shall not see life, you shall exist in eternal death, for the wrath of God cannot abide on a non-existent creature.

The Unbeliever's Unhappy Condition,
Volume 17, Sermon #1012 - John 3:36

If I believed that sinners could be annihilated I should have no particular reason for preaching to them; in fact, I should have a very urgent reason for never doing anything of the kind.

The Christian's Great Business,
Volume 19, Sermon #1130 - Psalm 51:12-13

Little will it abate our eternal misery if all the rest of the world should be lost with us; company in hell will be the reverse of consolation! If we lose heaven for fashion's sake it will be no solace to us that others lost it too.

Decision-Illustrated by the Case of Joshua,
Volume 21, Sermon #1229 - Joshua 24:15

Time tries most things, but eternity tries all.

The King's Weighings,
Volume 29, Sermon #1736 - 1 Samuel 2:3

If you were now in hell, you would have no cause to complain against the justice of God, for you deserves to be there.

Pleading, Not Contradicting,
Volume 36, Sermon #2129 - Matthew 15:27

Eternal life commences here; it begins in the believer as soon as he is born again. Then he receives unto him that same life which he will have throughout eternity.

Eternal Life!,
Volume 41, Sermon #2396 - John 17:3, 1 John 5:20, 21

You need not to know much about Heaven—it is where Christ is, and that is Heaven enough for us.

The Rule and Reward of Serving Christ,
Volume 42, Sermon #2449 - John 12:26.

I shall never understand, even in Heaven, why the Lord Jesus should ever have loved me.

Love's Vigilance Rewarded,
Volume 42, Sermon #2485 - Song of Solomon 3:4

To go anywhere without our God is terrible—but to die without the Presence of God would be awful beyond expression.

Moving,
Volume 48, Sermon #2811 - Exodus 33:15

"To glorify God and to enjoy Him forever" is the only worthy end of mortal man!

Barriers Obliterated,
Volume 49, Sermon #2847 - Isaiah 44:22

I do believe that there are some Christians whom God himself will never satisfy until he takes them to heaven.

Owl or Eagle?,
Volume 49, Sermon #2860 - Psalm 102:6, Psalm 103:5

It is not said in Heaven, "Moral, moral, moral are You, O God!" But, "Holy, holy, holy are You, O Lord!"

Holiness Demanded,
Volume 50, Sermon #2902 - Hebrews 12:14

In these busy times, when men have so much to do in order to live, it may be of much service to them to think how certainly they must die.

A Challenge and War Cry,
Volume 51, Sermon #2929 - 1 Corinthians 15:55-58

Death has no sting to a Believer. Once death was the penalty of sin—sin being forgiven, the penalty ceases and Christians do not die, now, as a punishment for their sin, but they die that they may be prepared to live!

A Challenge and War Cry,
Volume 51, Sermon #2929 - 1 Corinthians 15:55-58

Almost saved is altogether lost! There are many in Hell who once were almost saved, but who are now altogether damned. Think of that, you who are not far from the Kingdom. It is being in the Kingdom that saves the soul, not being near the Kingdom.

Near the Kingdom, Or in It?,
Volume 52, Sermon #2989 - Mark 12:34

My testimony is that if I had to die like a dog. If this life were all and there were no hereafter, I would prefer to be a Christian for the joy and peace which, in this present life, godliness will afford.

Silken Cords,
Volume 52, Sermon #3005 - Hosea 11:4

The pains of the damned in Hell are no atonement for sin! They suffer in consequence of sin, but no atonement has been made by them, for all they have suffered has not lessened what they have to suffer. And when ten thousand times ten thousand years shall have rolled over their poor accursed heads, they will be just as far off having satisfied Divine Justice as they are now, for sin is such a dreadful thing that even Tophet cannot burn it up, though "the pile thereof is fire and much wood," and though "the breath of the Lord, like a stream of brimstone, does kindle it." Sin is cast into its flames and men suffer there—but all the burnings of Gehenna never did consume a single sin, and never could. Think of that! Earth, Heaven and Hell could never take away a single sin from a single soul!

The Guilt and the Cleansing,
Volume 53, Sermon #3056 - Psalm 51:7

There is no sleep in Hell. Oh, what a blessing sleep would be if it could enter the habitation of the damned!

An Observation of the Preacher,
Volume 53, Sermon #3072 - Ecclesiastes 7:8

Our present actions are not trifles, for they will decide our everlasting destiny. Everything we do is, to some extent, a sowing of which eternity will be the reaping.

Sowing and Reaping,
Volume 54, Sermon #3109 - Galatians 6:7

I have not the least particle of faith in rambling spirits. Those who are in Heaven will not care to be wandering in these foggy regions! and those in Hell cannot leave their dread abode.

Good Cheer from Christ's Real Presence,
Volume 55, Sermon #3128 - Mark 6:45-52

If any man can say, "I am sure of Heaven, and I am proud of it," he may take my word for it that he is secure of Hell! If your religion puffs you up, puff your religion away, for it is not worth a puff!

The Hope That Purifies,
Volume 57, Sermon #3235 - 1 John 3:3

I must frankly confess that of all my expectations of Heaven, I will cheerfully renounce ten thousand things if I can but know that I shall have perfect holiness, for if I may become like Jesus Christ as to His Character—pure and perfect—I cannot understand how any other joy can be denied me! If we shall have that, surely we shall have everything! This, then, is our hope—that "we shall be like He, for we shall see Him as He is."

The Hope That Purifies,
Volume 57, Sermon #3235 - 1 John 3:3

Those who expect to find the road to Heaven smooth and unobstructed will discover little in the experience of the ancient saints to support the expectation.

Woe and Weal,
Volume 57, Sermon #3239 - Micah 7:9

Heaven is a place and state of perfect rest, yet it is not the rest of silence and stagnation! In one sense, they rest not day nor night, yet they serve God continually—and that is perfect rest!

The Lord's Eternal Rest,
Volume 58, Sermon #3294 - Psalm 132:14

Whenever you can see Christ's hand in it, it makes the bitter sweet and heavy things soon grow light! Go to your sickbed as you hope to go to your deathbed—through the Door, that is, through Christ.

The Only Door,
Volume 58, Sermon #3287 - John 10:9

Evangelism

A sinner has a heart as well as a head; a sinner has emotions as well as thoughts; and we must appeal to both. A sinner will never be converted until his emotions are stirred.

The Soul Winner, Page 22

You must go into the fire if you are to pull others out of it, and you will have to dive into the floods if you are to draw others out of the water.

The Soul Winner, Page 200

If you really long to save men's souls, you must tell them a great deal of disagreeable truth.

Words of Counsel, Page 15

If we had to preach to thousands year after year, and never rescued but one soul, that one soul would be a full reward for all our labour, for a soul is of countless price.

Wanted, A Guest Chamber!,
Volume 13, Sermon #785 - Mark 14:14

Soul-winning keeps the heart lively, and preserves our warm youth to us; it is a mighty refresher to decaying love.

"By All Means, Save Some",
Volume 20, Sermon #1170 - 1 Corinthians 9:22

He who never seeks the conversion of another is in imminent danger of being damned himself.

Conversions Desired,
Volume 22, Sermon #1282 - Acts 11:21

You must not imagine that in this church all who have come to Christ nominally have come really.

Gathering to the Center,
Volume 22, Sermon #1298 - Mark 1:45

Do you want to go to heaven alone? I fear you will never go there. Have you no wish for others to be saved? Then you are not saved yourself. Be sure of that.

"She Was Not Hid,"
Volume 34, Sermon #2019 - Luke 8:47

There is somebody in the world whom you have to bring to Christ. I do not know where he is, or who he is; but you had better look out for him.

Paul Apprehended and Apprehending,
Volume 39, Sermon #2315 - Philippians 3:12

Brethren, if you were to go to heaven now, perhaps you would go almost alone; but you must stop till there is a companion to go with you.

The Sojourn in Mesech,
Volume 48, Sermon #2780 - Psalm 120:5

But if you should not live to see it on earth, remember you are only accountable for your labour, and not for your success.

Harvest Time,
Volume 50, Sermon #2896 - 1 Samuel 12:17

Our converts are worth nothing. If they are converted by man they can be unconverted by man.

Election—Its Defenses and Evidences,
Volume 51, Sermon #2920 - 1 Thessalonians 1:4-6

Beware, beloved, of all dry-eyed reformations.

"Going and Weeping,"
Volume 53, Sermon #3049 - Jeremiah 50:4

You will win as many souls as God gives you, but no one will be converted by your own power.

The Commissariat of the Universe,
Volume 55, Sermon #3149 - Psalm 104:28

Evolution

The worst sort of clever men are those who know better than the Bible and are so learned that they believe that the world had no Maker, and that men are only monkeys with their tails rubbed off.

John Ploughman's Pictures, Page 84

You cannot convince the simplest boy in the street that somehow or other he was developed from an oyster, or some creature inferior to that, and yet these profound thinkers bow down to such a belief as this.

The Two Yokes,
Volume 18, Sermon #1032 - Jeremiah 28:13

Speak of evolution—here it is—"When lust has conceived, it brings forth sin: and sin, when it is finished, brings forth death." Darkness never begets light, filth never creates purity, hell never yields heaven, and depravity never produces grace.

The Singular Origin of a Christian,
Volume 31, Sermon #1829 - Ephesians 2:10

Within fifty years children in the school will read of extraordinary popular delusions, and this will be mentioned as one of the most absurd of them.

Hideous Discovery,
Volume 32, Sermon #1911 - Mark 7:20-23

If God's word be true, evolution is a lie.

Hideous Discovery,
Volume 32, Sermon #1911 - Mark 7:20-23

If those who believed in evolution said their prayers rightly, they would begin them with, "Our Father, which art up a tree."

Idols Found Wanting, But Jehovah Found Faithful,
Volume 34, Sermon #2056 - Isaiah 46:1-4

Faith

Faith obliterates time, annihilates distance, and brings future things at once into its possession.

According to Promise, Page 52

He would have us like children who believe what their father tells them.

An All Around Ministry, Page 330

Faith is the fountain, the foundation and the fosterer of obedience.

Barbed Arrows, Page 88

Faith laughs at that which fear weeps over.

Barbed Arrows, Page 88

Faith trades in marvels, and her merchandise is with wonders.

The Soul Winner, Page 154

We are not to look to what we have. The witness of the senses only confuses those who would walk by faith.

Words of Counsel, Page 52

Now, I hold no man's faith to be sure faith unless he knows what he believes.

Faith,
Volume 3, Sermon #107 - Hebrews 11:6

The world hangs on nothing; but faith cannot hang upon itself, it must hang on Christ.

The Blood,
Volume 5, Sermon #228 - Exodus 12:13

Faith is both God's gift and man's act. The Lord is the author of our faith, but we ourselves believe.

Strong Faith,
Volume 23, Sermon #1367 - Romans 4:20

Faith receives more stabs from waverers than from avowed skeptics.

Great Spoil,
Volume 28, Sermon #1641 - Psalm 119:162

Faith is led confidently to expect what reason would never suggest.

God the Wonder-Worker,
Volume 33, Sermon #1981 - Psalm 136:4

Faith is the linen which binds the plaster of Christ's reconciliation to the sore of our sin.

Number 2000-Or, "Healing By the Stripes of Jesus",
Volume 33, Sermon #2000

Faith is the linen which binds the plaster of Christ's reconciliation to the sore of our sin.

Number 2000-Or, "Healing By the Stripes of Jesus",
Volume 33, Sermon #2000

My Lord gives me unlimited credit at the Bank of Faith.

Pleading, Not Contradicting,
Volume 36, Sermon #2129 - Matthew 15:27

If you truly believe in Jesus, it is for life. Saving faith is a life-long act.

Believing on Jesus-and Its Counterfeits,
Volume 37, Sermon #2191 - John 8:30-32

Faith is sanctified common-sense.

Sealed and Open Evidences,
Volume 39, Sermon #2297 - Jeremiah 32:14

Every Divine promise, if it is rightly viewed by faith, will make the heart leap for joy.

God Has Spoken!-Rejoice!,
Volume 50, Sermon #2864 - Psalm 108:7

Until a man receives faith, he may think that he has it—but when he has real faith in Jesus Christ, then he shudders as he thinks how long he has lived in unbelief—and realizes how much of unbelief is still mixed with his belief.

Feeble Faith Appealing to A Strong Savior,
Volume 50, Sermon #2881 - Mark 9:24

After faith comes repentance, or, rather, repentance is faith's twin brother and is born at the same time.

forgiveness and Fear,
Volume 50, Sermon #2882 - Psalm 130:4

Faith in the storm is true faith! Faith in a calm may be, or may not be, genuine faith.

An Instructive Truth,
Volume 50, Sermon #2893 - Jeremiah 10:23

Faith is the channel of salvation, not the fountain and source of it.

The Search Warrant,
Volume 50, Sermon #2898 - John 6:64

That faith which is not accompanied by repentance will have to be repented of!

The Plumb Line,
Volume 50, Sermon #2904 - Amos 7:7, 8

If we begin by doubting, our prayer will limp. Faith is the tendon of Achilles and if that is cut, it is not possible for us to wrestle with God.

The Singing Army!,
Volume 51, Sermon #2923 - 2 Chronicles 20:4

Faith is the accepting of what God gives. Faith is the believing what God says. Faith is the trusting to what Jesus has done. Only do this and you are saved, as surely as you are alive!

False Justification and True,
Volume 51, Sermon #2932 - Job 9:20, Romans 8:33, 34

No faith brings greater glory to God than the faith of the audaciously guilty when they dare to believe that God can forgive them!

Great Changes,
Volume 51, Sermon #2934 - Luke 13:30

It is not the strength of your faith that saves you, but the strength of Him upon whom you rely! Christ is able to save you if you come to Him—be your faith weak or be it strong.

The Big Gates Wide Open,
Volume 51, Sermon #2954 - John 6:37

It is possible for even a good man to fail one who trusts him, but it is quite impossible for God to fail the soul that has relied upon Him.

Power with God,
Volume 52, Sermon #2978 - Genesis 32:28

The result of faith and confession is salvation.

Faith First, Confession Following,
Volume 52, Sermon #3011 - Romans 10:10

Though your faith is no bigger than a mustard seed, so that you can hardly see it, it will bring salvation to you! Even if you cannot see it, God can. If you do but touch the hem of Christ's garment, virtue will flow out of Him to the saving of your soul!

Enquiring the Way of Zion,
Volume 53, Sermon #3035 - Jeremiah 50:5

What a mercy it is for us that God does not judge us by our hasty speeches! If He can see only a spark of faith amidst the dense smoke of our unbelief, He accepts it!

Faith Justifying Speech,
Volume 56, Sermon #3200 - Psalm 116:10

Faith is a principle which has its root deeper than feelings. We believe, whether we see or not. We believe, whether we feel or not.

Our Leader through the Darkness,
Volume 59, Sermon #3370 - Isaiah 50:10, Isaiah 55:4

It takes much more faith to be an unbeliever than to be a believer.

Are You Mocked?,
Volume 62, Sermon #3512 - Psalm 14:6

False Teaching

Every grace can be counterfeited, even as jewels can be imitated.

According to Promise, Page 3

"Is your father a Christian?" said a Sunday-school teacher to a child. The girl answered, "Yes, I believe that father is a Christian; but he has not worked much at it lately." No doubt there are many of that sort. Their religion has taken a holiday, and they themselves have gone to a sluggard's bed. Let them be aroused, for it is high time to awaken out of sleep.

Barbed Arrows, Page 125

If you profess to be a Christian, yet find full satisfaction in worldly pleasures and pursuits, your profession is false.

Morning and Evening, Page 355

It very often happens that the converts that are born in excitement die when the excitement is over.

The Soul Winner, Page 16

Let them get home to their knees and pray God to give them

manliness enough at least to be damned honestly, and not go Down to perdition wearing the name of Christian when Christians they are not.

The Sieve,
Volume 20, Sermon #1158 - Matthew 7:21

The devil has more to do with some men's pitiless theology than they imagine.

The Leading of the Spirit, the Secret Token of the Sons of God,
Volume 21, Sermon #1220 - Romans 8:14

Nobody can do as much damage to the church of God as the man who is within its walls, but not within its life.

The Form of Godliness Without the Power,
Volume 35, Sermon #2089 - 2 Timothy 3:5

There are too many of our converts about; we may find them everywhere except in heaven; but woe unto the man who is content with being the convert of his fellow-man!

A Visit from the Lord,
Volume 44, Sermon #2599 - Psalm 106:4

Who, think you, are the more honest men,—those who tell you plainly what the Scriptures say concerning this wrath of God, or those who smooth it over, or deny it altogether?

"Flee from the Wrath to Come",
Volume 46, Sermon #2704 - Matthew 3:7, Hebrews 6:18

Why, these are sham Christians; they are not genuine Christians; they are of the world, and do the things of the world. We may conclude that their hearts and natures are worldly, for if they were spiritual they would love spiritual things, and their hearts would be engaged in spiritual exercises.

Deliverance from the Power of Darkness,
Volume 59, Sermon #3366 - Colossians 1:13

Family Life

I have sometimes met with a deeper spiritual experience in

children of ten and twelve than I have in certain persons of fifty and sixty. It is an old proverb that some children are born with beards.

Come Ye Children, Page 24

Do not hesitate to tell the child his ruin; he will not else desire the remedy. Tell him also of the punishment for sin, and warn him of its terror. Be tender, but true.

Come Ye Children, Page 71

Before you can teach children, you must get the silver key of kindness to unlock their hearts, and so secure their attention.

Come Ye Children, Page 84

Be sure, whatever you leave out, that you teach the children the three Rs,—Ruin, Redemption, and Regeneration.

Come Ye Children, Page 90

Begin early to teach, for children begin early to sin.

John Ploughman's Pictures, Page 69

Give to a pig when it grunts, and to a child when it cries, and you will have a fine pig and a spoiled child.

John Ploughman's Talk, Page 37

If we never have headaches through rebuking our little children, we shall have plenty of heartaches when they grow up.

John Ploughman's Talk, Page 38

Never promise a child and then fail to perform, whether you promise him a bun or a beating.

John Ploughman's Talk, Page 38

To keep debt, dirt, and the devil out of my cottage has been my greatest wish ever since I set up housekeeping; and although the last of the three has sometimes got in by the door or the window, for the old serpent will wriggle through the smallest crack, yet thanks to a good wife, hard work, honesty, and scrubbing brushes, the two others have not crossed the threshold.

John Ploughman's Talk, Page 77

Home is the grandest of all institutions.

John Ploughman's Talk, Page 95

To reclaim the prodigal is well, but to save him from ever being a prodigal is better.

Words of Counsel, Page 126

For my part, I am more and more persuaded that the study of a good Scriptural catechism is of infinite value to our children, and I shall see that it is reprinted as cheaply as possible for your use. Even if the youngsters do not understand all the questions and answers in the "Westminster Assembly's Catechism," yet, abiding in their memories, it will be of infinite service when the time of understanding comes, to have those very excellent, wise, and judicious definitions of the things of God. If we would maintain orthodoxy in our midst, and see good old Calvinistic doctrines handed down from father to son, I think we must use the method of catechizing, and endeavor with all our might to impregnate their minds with the things of God.

A Promise for Us and for Our Children,
Volume 10, Sermon #564 - Isaiah 44:1-5

To bury a child is a great grief, but to have that child live and sin against you is ten times worse.

Secret Sins Driven Out By Stinging Hornets,
Volume 12, Sermon #673 - Deuteronomy 7:20

If you are professing Christians, but cannot say that you have no greater joy than the conversion of your children, you have reason to question whether you ought to have made such a profession at all.

The Parent's and Pastor's Joy,
Volume 19, Sermon #1148 - 3 John, 4

Our fathers are all very well—God bless them!—and a father's godly influence and earnest prayers are of untold value to his children; but the mothers are worth two of them, mostly, as to the moral training and religious bent of their sons and daughters.

Young Man! A Prayer for You,
Volume 37, Sermon #2215 - 2 Kings 6:17

If you have no family prayer and your children do not grow up to be Christians, how can you expect that they will?

Bringing Sinners to the Savior,
Volume 47, Sermon #2731 - Mark 9:17-20

The preacher ought to preach so that it shall be almost an impossibility for his hearer to be altogether careless. You Christian people should set such an example in your households that it shall be next door to an impossibility for son or daughter or servant to remain at peace while they remain out of God and out of Christ in a state of sin!

Sham Conversion,
Volume 51, Sermon #2928 - 2 Kings 17:25, 33, 34

Now, if you pray in one way with your lips and in another way with your lives, your lives will win the day and your children will rather be like what you are than what you ask for them to be.

Too Little for the Lamb,
Volume 51, Sermon #2937 - Exodus 12:3, 4

Sweet above all other things is love—a mother's love, a father's love, a husband's love, a wife's love—but all these are only faint images of the love of God!

"His Great Love",
Volume 52, Sermon #2968 - Ephesians 2:4, 5

Sweet above all other things is love—a mother's love, a father's love, a husband's love, a wife's love—but all these are only faint images of the love of God!

"His Great Love",
Volume 52, Sermon #2968 - Ephesians 2:4, 5

It is no unusual thing for a little child to be the god of the family—and wherever that is the case, there is a rod laid up in store in that house. You cannot make idols of your children without finding out, sooner or later, that God makes them into rods with which He will punish you for your idolatry!

Fifteen Years After!,
Volume 53, Sermon #3025 - Job 1:21

I know that the words of my father with me alone, when he prayed for me, and bade me pray for myself,—not to use any form of prayer, but to pray just as I felt, and to ask from God what I felt that I really wanted,—left an impression upon my mind that will never be erased.

The Sparrow and the Swallow,
Volume 53, Sermon #3041 - Psalm 84:3

Every Christian should think that what is good for himself is good for his children! He who does not labor and pray for the salvation of his own offspring has good reason to doubt whether he knows the Grace of God, himself.

The Sparrow and the Swallow,
Volume 53, Sermon #3041 - Psalm 84:3

The objective of parents, preachers and teachers should be that children should be saved while they are children!

The Sparrow and the Swallow,
Volume 53, Sermon #3041 - Psalm 84:3

How glad I am when I can receive husband and wife into the Church at the same time! and I am still more glad when there is a little train of their sons and daughters behind them all coming together to confess their faith in Christ!

Lessons from A Dovecot,
Volume 53, Sermon #3051 - Isaiah 60:8

It is really scandalous when nurses and others tell little children idle tales and foolish stories which the children believe to be true. We should be very careful and jealous concerning the faith which a little child has in its elders and never do or say anything to weaken their belief.

Idolatry Condemned,
Volume 53, Sermon #3071 - 1 John 5:21

Oh, do make your households to be like flower gardens—plant no thorns and root out all ill weeds of discontent! Depend upon it, household happiness is a great means of promoting household holiness!

A Pastoral Visit,
Volume 54, Sermon #3103 - Philemon 1:2

There are some households where all are saved—how happy they should be!—where every son and every daughter, father, and mother are all believers—a church in the house, a church of which the whole of the house is comprised. It is such an unspeakable blessing that those who enjoy it ought never to cease to praise God for it day and night.

Household Sin and Sorrow,
Volume 61, Sermon #3473 - Genesis 27:35

I am sure we cannot expect our children to grow up a godly seed if there is no family prayer.

Daniel-A Pattern for Pleaders,
Volume 61, Sermon #3484 - Daniel 9:19

Brethren, if you wish to give your children a blessing when you die, be a blessing to them while you live. If you would make your last words worth the hearing, let your whole life be worth the seeing.

A Remarkable Benediction,
Volume 62, Sermons #3540 - Deuteronomy 33:16

Fear

Fear is not a mean motive; it is a very proper motive for a guilty man to feel.

Sight for Those Who See Not,
Volume 30, Sermon #1798 - John 9:39

Half our fears are the result of ignorance.

Earthquake But Not Heartquake,
Volume 33, Sermon #1950 - Psalm 46:1-3

Half our fears arise from neglect of the Bible.

Folly of Unbelief,
Volume 33, Sermon #1980 - Luke 24:25

It is not what we see that we dread, so much as that which we do not see, and therefore exaggerate.

The Child of Light Walking in Darkness,
Volume 33, Sermon #1985 - Isaiah 50:10

Some of you dare not do a thing that you know to be right, because somebody might make a remark about it. What are you but slaves?

"Christ Is All",
Volume 50, Sermon #2888 - Colossians 3:11

As for me, I have braved the sneer of men because I feared the frown of my Lord.

Jerusalem the Guilty,
Volume 62, Sermon #3520 - Luke 13:33

Fellowship

The converse of saints on earth should be a rehearsal of their everlasting communion in heaven.

The Bridegroom's Parting Words,
Volume 29, Sermon #1716 - Song of Solomon 8:13

Some Christians try to go to heaven alone, in solitude; but believers are not compared to bears, or lions, or other animals that wander alone; but those who belong to Christ are sheep in this respect, that they love to get together. Sheep go in flocks, and so do God's people.

A Call to the Lord's Own Flock,
Volume 30, Sermon #1807 - Ezekiel 34:30, 31

Warm-hearted saints keep each other warm, but cold is also contagious.

The Search for Faith,
Volume 33, Sermon #1963 - Luke 18:8

If any of you are in positions where you can enjoy Christian fellowship, and you have an opportunity of earning ten times as much money in another position where you must give up that fellowship, do not do it.

Christians Kept from Sin,
Volume 53, Sermon #3037 - 1 Samuel 25:32, 33

Let us treasure the virtues and excellences of our fellow-members, and search for signs of the Spirit's work in them; and, remembering our own imperfections and failures, let us not fix our eyes upon their defects.

"In Remembrance",
Volume 55, Sermon #3130 - 1 Corinthians 11:24, 25

Finances

Small shoes are apt to pinch, but not if you have a small foot; if we have little means it will be well to have little desires. Poverty is no shame, but being discontented with it is.

John Ploughman's Talk, Page 42

It is not how much we have, but how much we enjoy that brings happiness.

John Ploughman's Talk, Page 43

Poverty is hard, but debt is horrible.

John Ploughman's Talk, Page 78

If you want to sleep soundly, buy a bed of a man who is in debt; surely it must be a very soft one, or he never could have rested so easy on it.

John Ploughman's Talk, Page 82

Scripture says, "Owe no man anything," which does not mean pay your debts, but never have any to pay.

John Ploughman's Talk, Page 83

Men do not become rich by what they get, but by what they save.

John Ploughman's Talk, Page 110

Even crumbs are bread.

John Ploughman's Talk, Page 140

Money has wings of its own, and if you find it another pair of wings, wonder not if it flies fast.

John Ploughman's Talk, Page 146

I have heard of some good old woman in a cottage, who had nothing but a piece of bread and a little water, and lifting up her hands, she said, as a blessing, "What! all this, and Christ too?"

The Peculiar Sleep of the Beloved,
Volume 1, Sermon #12 - Psalm 127:2

As to money, every man will have enough when he has a little more, but contentment with his gains comes to no man.

The Overflowing Cup,
Volume 21, Sermon #1222 - Psalm 23:5

When the vulture of dissatisfaction has once fixed its talons in the breast it will not cease to tear at your vitals.

Spiritual Appetite,
Volume 21, Sermon #1227 - Proverbs 27:7

To many men it is given to have all that heart can wish, and yet not to have what their heart does wish. They have everything except contentment.

Beware of Unbelief,
Volume 21, Sermon #1238 - 2 Kings 7:2

Godly poverty is better than unhallowed riches.

The Singing Pilgrim,
Volume 28, Sermon #1652 - Psalm 119:54

If religion does not make you richer, which it may not do, it will make you more contented with what you have.

A Straight Talk,
Volume 36, Sermon #2122 - Luke 14:2

Ah, dear friends, God has only to give you what you want, to make you feel the emptiness of it! If you are his child, the more you have the less you will see in it.

A Clarion Call to Saints and Sinners,
Volume 37, Sermon #2225 - Micah 2:10

God has said he will never leave us, and if we have him we possess all things. Who has need to be covetous when all things are his, and God is his?

A New Year's Benediction,
Volume 60, Sermon #3387 - Hebrews 13:5

Free Will

When we shall see the dead rise from the grave by their own power, then may we expect to see ungodly sinners of their own free will turning to Christ.

Morning and Evening, Page 505

They who think that predestination and the fulfillment of the divine purpose is contrary to the free-agency of man, know not what they say, nor whereof they affirm. It were no miracle for God to effect his own purpose, if he were dealing with stocks and stones, with granite and with trees; but this is the miracle of miracles, that the creatures are free, absolutely free, and the divine purpose stands! Herein is wisdom!

The Infallibility of God's Purpose,
Volume 7, Sermon #406 - Job 23:13

Every creature free and doing as it wills, yet God more free still and doing as he wills, not only in heaven but among the inhabitants of this lower earth.

The Infallibility of God's Purpose,
Volume 7, Sermon #406 - Job 23:13

Despite all the doctrines which proud free-will has manufactured, there has never been found from Adam's day until now a single instance in which the sinner first sought his God. God must first seek him.

God's First Words to the First Sinner,
Volume 7, Sermon #412 - Genesis 3:9

According to the freewill scheme the Lord intends good, but he must wait like a lackey on his own creature to know what his intention is; God wills good and would do it, but he cannot, because he has an unwilling man who will not have God's good thing carried into effect. What do ye, sirs, but drag the eternal from his throne, and lift up into it that fallen creature, man; for man, according to that theory, nods, and his nod is destiny.

God's Will and Man's Will,
Volume 8, Sermon #442 - Romans 9:16, Revelation 22:17

Free-will doctrine—what does it? It magnifies man into God; it declares God's purposes a nullity, since they cannot be carried out unless men are willing. It makes God's will a waiting servant to the will of man, and the whole covenant of grace dependent upon human action. Denying election on the ground of injustice it holds God to be a debtor to sinners, so that if he gives grace to one he is bound to do so to all. It teaches that the blood of Christ was shed equally for all men, and since some are lost, this doctrine ascribes the difference to man's own will, thus making the atonement itself a powerless thing until the will of man gives it efficacy.

A Jealous God,
Volume 9, Sermon #502 - Exodus 34:14

It seems inexplicable to me that those who claim free will so very boldly for man, should not also allow some free will to God.

The Relationship of Marriage,
Volume 13, Sermon #762 - Jeremiah 3:14

Certain of my brethren are much taken up with the fact of man's free agency. I believe that he is a free agent, but it is only by his free agency that he is lost.

Others to Be Gathered In,
Volume 24, Sermon #1437 - Isaiah 56:8

Whatever may be said about freewill as a theory, it is never found as a matter of fact that any man, left to himself, ever woos his God, or pines after friendship with his Maker.

"Herein Is Love",
Volume 29, Sermon #1707 - 1 John 4:10, 11

"Oh," says one, "but men are free agents." I never thought that they were not, although I am not sure that it is much to their gain that they are. The glorious privilege of the freedom of the will has been terribly overrated: it is a dangerous heritage which has already lost us Paradise, and will lose us all hope of heaven unless the mighty grace of God shall interpose.

Strength and Recovery,
Volume 30, Sermon #1805 - Zechariah 10:12

"Well," saith one, "have not men a free-will?" Certainly, and the wonder is that free grace does not violate it, and yet the purpose of God is accomplished. Free-will alone ruins men; but free-will guided by free grace is another matter.

The Very Bold Prophecy,
Volume 32, Sermon #1919 - Isaiah 65:1

I never yet knew anybody repent who gloried in his power to repent; I never yet knew a man heart-broken for sin who boasted that he could break his own heart when and where he pleased.

A Paradox,
Volume 34, Sermon #2050 - 2 Corinthians 12:10

That is the sternest blow against free-will of which I know; what a free- willer can make out of that text, I cannot tell. He says that any man can come to Christ, yet Christ said to some, "Ye will not come to me;" and both observation and experience prove that this is still true. Never yet did a soul come to Christ till first Christ came to it.

New Tokens of Ancient Love,
Volume 50, Sermon #2880 - Jeremiah 31:3

Any man who should deny that man is a free agent might well be thought unreasonable, but free-will is a different thing from free-agency.

Election—It's Defenses and Evidences,
Volume 51, Sermon #2920 - 1 Thessalonians 1:4-6

The fact is, brethren, there is a predestination, and the doctrines of election and effectual grace are true, nor may we deny them; but yet the Lord deals with men as responsible beings, and bids them "strive to enter in at the strait gate," and to "lay hold on eternal life." Such exhortations are evidently intended for free agents, and indicate that our salvation requires energetic action.

The Commissariat of the Universe,
Volume 55, Sermon #3149 - Psalm 104:28

There is no greater mockery than to call a sinner a free man. Show me a convict toiling in the chain gang, and call him a free man if you will; point out to me the galley slave chained to the oar, and smarting under the taskmaster's lash whenever he pauses to draw breath, and call him a free man if you will; but never call a sinner a free man, even in his will, so long as he is the slave of his own corruptions. In our natural state, we wore chains, not upon our limbs, but upon our hearts, fetters that bound us, and kept us from God, from rest, from peace, from holiness, from anything like freedom of heart and conscience and will. The iron entered into our soul; and there is no slavery as terrible as that. As there is no freedom like the freedom of the spirit, so is there no slavery that is at all comparable to the bondage of the heart.

The Blood of Christ's Covenant,
Volume 57, Sermon #3240 - Zechariah 9:11

Friendship

A friend to everybody is often a friend to nobody.

John Ploughman's Talk, Page 34

If we would always recollect that we live among men who are imperfect, we should not be in such a fever when we find out our friend's failings.

John Ploughman's Talk, Page 66

We are one in Christ; let us be friends with one another; but let us never be friends with one another's error. If I be wrong, rebuke me sternly; I can bear it, and bear it cheerfully; and if ye be wrong, expect the like measure from me, and neither peace nor parley with your mistakes.

War! War! War!,
Volume 5, Sermon #250 - 1 Samuel 18:17

One heart in two bodies is the realization of true brotherhood.

the Lord's Own View of His Church and People,
Volume 33, Sermon #1957 - Song of Solomon 4:12

It is no friendship that flatters; it is small friendship that holds its tongue when it ought to speak; but it is true friendship that can speak a word at the right time, and, if need be, even speak so sharply as to cause a wound.

The Best Friend,
Volume 45, Sermon #2627 - Proverbs 27:10

Gifts

There is no person without a talent of some sort or other, no one without some form of power either given by nature or acquired by education. We are all endowed in some degree or other, and we must each one give an account for that talent.

We Endeavor, Page 50

'Every good gift and every perfect gift is from above'—nothing from human nature, nothing from mere free agency. Good and perfect gifts are flowers too rich and rare to spring up of themselves upon the dunghill of human nature.

"A Kind of First Fruits",
Volume 57, Sermon #3275 - James 1:18

Giving

Feel for others—in your pocket

John Ploughman's Talk, Page 8

Honesty first, and then generosity.

John Ploughman's Talk, Page 86

He who tries to cheat the Lord will be quite ready to cheat his fellow men.

John Ploughman's Talk, Page 136

Giving is true having, as the old gravestone said of the dead man, "What I spent I had, what I saved I lost, what I gave I have."

John Ploughman's Talk, Page 147

Our gifts are not to be measured by the amount we contribute, but by the surplus kept in our own hand.

the Best Donation,
Volume 37, Sermon #2234 - 2 Corinthians 8:5

Glory

Our Lord's great object in laying down his life upon the cross was the father's glory.

Good News for Seekers,
Volume 22, Sermon #1312 - Psalm 22:26.

Surely he is the grandest creature God has made who glorifies him most.

A Golden Prayer,
Volume 24, Sermon #1391 - John 12:28

We endeavor to glorify him now by our actions, but then he will be glorified in our own persons, and character, and condition. He is glorified by what we do, but he is at the last to be glorified in what we are.

Jesus Admired in Them That Believe,
Volume 25, Sermon #1477 - 2 Thessalonians 1:10

If God be glorified, does it really matter where we are? What becomes of us is of small consequence compared with bringing glory to his great name.

"The King Can Do No Wrong",
Volume 41, Sermon #2420 - 2 Samuel 3:36

The salvation of men is a grand aim, but it must always be in subordination to the glory of the Lord, that his arm may be revealed, and that all flesh may see it together.

The Lord's Knowledge, Our Safeguard,
Volume 41, Sermon #2441 - 2 Peter 2:9

The first thought of the truly blessed man is how he can best glorify the name of Christ and in so doing he avoids "the counsel of the ungodly."

The Truly Blessed Man,
Volume 57, Sermon #3270 - Psalm 1:1-3

God the Father

Hide nothing from him, for you can hide nothing.

The Treasury of David,
Psalms 62, Verse 8

God knows us before we know anything.

The Treasury of David,
Psalms 71, Verse 6

It is taken for granted by all theologians that God can neither suffer nor feel. There is no such thing in the Word of God.

God's First Words to the First Sinners,
Volume 7, Sermon #412 - Genesis 3:9

He never loves them less, he cannot love them more.

The Perfuming of the Heart,
Volume 14, Sermon #829 - Romans 5:5

He is the happy God, and would have those round about him happy.

Fresh Grace Confidently Expected,
Volume 19, Sermon #1122 - Psalm 92:10

Remember that thought is speech before God.

The Final Separation,
Volume 21, Sermon #1234 - Matthew 25:32

O think, that he who was master of all heaven's majesty came down to be the victim of all man's misery!

A Vindication of the Doctrine of Justification By Faith,
Volume 21, Sermon #1239 - Galatians 5:24

Brethren, we have two faults. We do not think God to be so great as he is, and we do not think God can be so little as he can be. We err on both sides, and neither know his height of glory nor his depth of grace.

At School,
Volume 26, Sermon #1519 - Psalm 143:10

Christ did not die to make his Father loving, but because his Father is loving: the atoning blood is the outflow of the very heart of God toward us.

"Love and I"—A Mystery,
Volume 28, Sermon #1667 - John 17:26

God would not even for mercy's sake issue an unjust pardon to the souls he loved.

Israel and Britain—A Note of Warning,
Volume 31, Sermon #1844 - John 12:37-41

The God of the past has blotted out your sin, the God of the present makes all things work for your good, the God of the future will never leave you nor forsake you.

The Master Key—Opening the Gate of Heaven,
Volume 33, Sermon #1938 - Genesis 32:12

His circumference is nowhere, but his centre is everywhere.

God's Nearness to Us,
Volume 33, Sermon #1973 - Acts 17:27

I dare say that we think that we magnify him, but in reality we belittle him with our highest thoughts.

"Is Anything Too Hard for the Lord?",
Volume 34, Sermon #2020 - Jeremiah 32:26, 27

Do you not know that his name is the happy God, and nothing gives him greater happiness then to give happiness to his creatures.

God Rejoicing in the New Creation,
Volume 37, Sermon #2211 - Isaiah 65:17-19

Come and take Christ—and you have found God. No man believes in Christ and remains without the favor of God.

Longing to Find God,
Volume 38, Sermon #2272 - Job 23:3

He can do anything that is right; but he cannot do a wrong thing.

No Fixity Without Faith,
Volume 39, Sermon #2305 - Isaiah 7:9

God thinks of every separate child of His as much as if He had only that one.

Lessons from the Manna,
Volume 39, Sermon #2332 - Exodus 16:4

He loved them, not for anything that he could ever gain from them, for he had all things in himself, but because of what he would impart to them.

Christ's Love to His Spouse,
Volume 42, Sermon #2488 - Ephesians 5:25

Everything of good that we enjoy, however little it may be, comes from God.

Jonah's Object-Lessons,
Volume 43, Sermon #2504 - Jonah 4:6-8.

It is congenial to God's Nature to make His creatures happy.

A Vexed Soul Comforted,
Volume 44, Sermon #2557 - Job 27:2

God's heart, not mine, is the measure of his giving; not my capacity to receive, but his capacity to give.

God's Heart the Source of All Blessing,
Volume 45, Sermon #2641 - 2 Samuel 7:21

He who counts the brilliant stars, counts such dim things as our understanding—and He who numbers the very hairs of our head never fails to reckon the cries of our hearts.

The Lesson of the Almond Tree,
Volume 46, Sermon #2678 - Jeremiah 1:11, 12

The least mercy from God is a miracle.

"Marvelous Loving Kindness",
Volume 46, Sermon #2702 - Psalm 17:7

We would be much more restful if we did but do our God the justice of trusting Him at all times, for He can never fail us!

"Return Unto Your Rest",
Volume 47, Sermon #2758 - Psalm 116:7

Surely a God whom we could understand would be no God!

God's Glory in Hiding Sin,
Volume 49, Sermon #2838 - Proverbs 25:2

The goodness of God to a man of evil life is not intended to encourage him to continue in his sin, but it is meant to woo and win him away from it.

God's Goodness Leading to Repentance,
Volume 49, Sermon #2857 - Romans 2:4

Theologians lay it down as an axiom that God cannot suffer, but I am not sure that they are right. I cannot understand God's love to me, I cannot rejoice as I should in his goodness to me unless I believe that the gift of his Son cost his heart divine and awful pangs. I know that I am treading upon delicate ground, and that I am standing where thick darkness gathers; but I am not certain that what theologians take for granted is necessarily true. That God can do everything, I do believe; and that, if he wills to suffer he can do so, I also believe.

The Saints' Riches,
Volume 56, Sermon #3204 - Romans 8:32

Distance is no distance in the sight of God.

Gathering in the Chosen,
Volume 58, Sermon #3308 - Jeremiah 31:8, 9

If we could understand God he would not be God, for it is a part of the nature of God that he should be infinitely greater than any created mind.

Are You Mocked?,
Volume 62, Sermon #3512 - Psalm 14:6

He began to create, he began actually to redeem, but he never began to love.

The Drawings of Love,
Volume 63, Sermon #3561 - Jeremiah 31:3

Good Works

Good works are not the root of faith, but they are its fruit.

Consulting with Jesus,
Volume 48, Sermon #2778 - 1 Kings 10:1-3

The results of good or evil deeds will abide forever and ever, so let us beware what we do since it can never be undone.

Believers A Blessing,
Volume 53, Sermon #3045 - Zechariah 8:13

Gospel

We have an unchanging gospel, which is not today green grass and tomorrow dry hay; but always the abiding truth of the immutable Jehovah.

Faith's Checkbook, August 31

Never lose heart in the power of the gospel. Do not believe that there exists any man, much less any race of men, for whom the gospel is not fitted.

The Cripple at Lystra,
Volume 10, Sermon #559 - Acts 14:9, 10

If God does not save men by truth, he certainly will not save them by lies. And if the old gospel is not competent to work a revival, then we will do without the revival.

Additions to the Church,
Volume 20, Sermon #1167 - Acts 2:47

The gospel does not come to us as a premium for virtue, but it presents us with forgiveness for sin. It is not a reward for health, but a medicine for sickness.

For Whom Did Christ Die?,
Volume 20, Sermon #1191 - Romans 5:6

No real faith was ever wrought in man by his own thoughts and imaginations; he must receive the gospel as a revelation from God, or he cannot receive it at all.

Forts Demolished and Prisoners Taken,
Volume 25, Sermon #1473 - 2 Corinthians 10:5

That which is new in theology is not true; the gospel was of full stature at its very birth; no man can add to it or take away from it.

God Glorified By Children's Mouths,
Volume 26, Sermon #1545 - Psalm 8:2

Nothing hardens like the gospel when it is long trifled with.

A Great Gospel for Great Sinners,
Volume 31, Sermon #1837 - 1 Timothy 1:15-17

The gospel is to precede and produce civilization.

"The Tender Mercy of Our God",
Volume 32, Sermon #1907 - Luke 1:77-79

The heart of the gospel is redemption, and the essence of redemption is the substitutionary sacrifice of Christ.

The Heart of the Gospel,
Volume 32, Sermon #1910 - 2 Corinthians 5:20, 21

Yes, if you accept the gospel you have found your God, but if you reject the gospel you have rejected God himself.

The Very Bold Prophecy,
Volume 32, Sermon #1919 - Isaiah 65:1

The true gospel is no new thing, it is as old as the hills.

The Curse and the Curse for Us,
Volume 35, Sermon #2093 - Galatians 3:10-14

And so, within the simple Gospel, how much lies concentrated? Look at it! Within that truth lie regeneration, repentance, faith, holiness, zeal, consecration, perfection. Heaven hides itself away within the Gospel.

The Mustard Seed-A Sermon for the Sunday School Teacher,
Volume 35, Sermon #2110 - Luke 13:18-19

The gospel is a gospel of giving and forgiving.

Praise for the Gift of Gifts,
Volume 38, Sermon #2247 - 2 Corinthians 9:15

Christ and His Gospel will always be spoken against. If you know a gospel which is approved by the age and patronized by the learned, that gospel is a lie!

Simeon's Swan Song,
Volume 39, Sermon #2293 - Luke 2:29, 30

Let this be to you the mark of true gospel preaching—where Christ is everything, and the creature is nothing; where it is salvation all of grace, through the work of the Holy Spirit applying to the soul the precious blood of Jesus.

The Cause and the Cure of a Wounded Spirit,
Volume 42, Sermon #2494 - Proverbs 18:14

We preach a gospel whose chief glory lies in the future.

Watching to See,
Volume 45, Sermon #2622 - Habakkuk 2:1-4

They love the Gospel most who know it best!

"Peace and Believing",
Volume 45, Sermon #2626 - Romans 15:13.

The same sun which melts wax hardens clay. And the same Gospel which melts some persons to repentance hardens others in their sins.

The Lesson of the Almond Tree,
Volume 46, Sermon #2678 - Jeremiah 1:11, 12

There are many points and particulars in which the Gospel is offensive to human nature and revolting to the pride of the creature. It was not intended to please man. How can we attribute such a purpose to God? Why should He devise a goal to suit the whims of our poor fallen human nature? He intended to save men, but He never intended to gratify their depraved tastes.

A Mournful Defection,
Volume 50, Sermon #2914 - John 6:67

You believe the Gospel is true, but you doubt whether it is for you. Well, no, it is not for you if you are not a sinner. If you can say, "I am not guilty," then farewell to all hope, for Jesus Christ came into the world to save sinners! If you are a sinner, surely He came to save such as you are!

Reasons for Doubting Christ,
Volume 51, Sermon #2925 - Matthew 14:31

Give me great sinners to make great saints! They are glorious raw material for Grace to work upon and when you do get them saved, they will shake the very gates of Hell!

Great Changes,
Volume 51, Sermon #2934 - Luke 13:30

What has the Gospel of Christ to do with education? You do not need a degree from a university—you do not need to be a master of arts, or bachelor of arts, in order to find Christ!

The Big Gates Wide Open,
Volume 51, Sermon #2954 - John 6:37

The invitations of the Gospel are invitations to happiness. In delivering God's message, we do not ask men to come to a funeral, but to a wedding feast!

"Marvelous Things",
Volume 54, Sermon #3086 - Psalm 98:1, 2

The great practical end of the Gospel is to bring the human heart into obedience to Christ and to make the stubborn will acknowledge allegiance to His sway.

Prompt Obedience,
Volume 58, Sermon #3310 - Psalm 18:44

Gossip

Hearsay is half lies. A tale never loses in the telling. As a snowball grows by rolling, so does a story. They who talk much lie much.

John Ploughman's Talk, Page 47

Grace

Grace is the mother and nurse of holiness, and not the apologist of sin.

Morning and Evening, Page 51

Grace does not make us unearthly, though it makes us unworldly.

Words of Counsel, Page 74

I take it that the highest proof of Christ's power is not that he offers salvation, not that he bids you take it if you will, but that when you reject it, when you hate it, when you despise it, he has a power whereby he can change your mind, make you think differently from your former thoughts, and turn you from the error of your ways.

A Mighty Savior,
Volume 3, Sermon #111 - Isaiah 63:1

A seat in heaven shall one day be yours; but a chain in hell would have been yours if grace had not changed you.

The Fruitless Vine,
Volume 3, Sermon #125 - Ezekiel 15:1, 2

No man is ever taken to heaven against his will, though I do not believe any man ever went there of his own free will till God's sovereign grace enlightened him and made him willing.

North and South,
Volume 17, Sermon #1007 - Isaiah 43:6

Give me the doctrines of grace, and I am in clover.

The Good Shepherdess,
Volume 19, Sermon #1119 - Song of Solomon 1:7, 8

Put the two truths together, that the love of God is first, and that the love of God is the cause of our love, and I think you will be inclined henceforth to be believers in what are commonly called the doctrines of grace.

Love's Birth and Parentage,
Volume 22, Sermon #1299 - 1 John 4:19

A man is very far gone in guilt when he reads grace the wrong way upwards, and infers, from the long suffering of the Lord, that he may continue in sin.

Return! Return!,
Volume 51, Sermon #2931 - Jeremiah 3:12, 14, 22

If God had begun saving us because we were good, he would of course leave off saving us when we were not good.

Paul's Parenthesis,
Volume 54, Sermon #3084 - 1 Corinthians 15:10

If grace does not make you to differ from your own surroundings, is it really grace at all?

Confession of Christ,
Volume 60, Sermon #3405 - Matthew 10:32, 33

Heart

The more objects you set your heart upon, the more thorns there are to tear your peace of mind to shreds.

The Friend of God,
Volume 33, Sermon #1962 - Isaiah 41:8, James 2:23

That which is down in the heart will come up into the mouth—and you may rest assured that men are fairly judged by the common current of their conversation.

Facts and Inferences,
Volume 57, Sermon #3232 - Psalm 37:35-37

Heaven

Thy head may be crowned with thorny troubles now, but it shall wear a starry crown ere long; thy hand may be filled with cares—it shall sweep the strings of the harp of heaven soon.

Morning and Evening, Page 268

In heaven they marry not, but are as the angels of God; yet there is this one marvelous exception to the rule, for in heaven Christ and His Church shall celebrate their joyous nuptials. This affinity as it is more lasting, so it is more near than earthly wedlock. Let the love of husband be never so pure and fervent, it is but a faint picture of the flame which burns in the heart of Jesus.

Morning and Evening, Page 408

The damnation of sinners shall not mar the happiness of saints.

The Treasury of David, Psalms 58, Verse 10

The rougher the voyage the more the mariners long for port, and heaven becomes more and more "a desired haven," as our trials multiply.

The Treasury of David, Psalms 107, Verse 30

I believe that heaven is a fellowship of the saints, and that we shall know one another there.

Heaven and Hell,
Volume 1, Sermon #39, 40 - Matthew 8:11, 12

There cannot be heaven without Christ. He is the sum total of bliss; the fountain from which heaven flows, the element of which heaven is composed. Christ is heaven and heaven is Christ.

"Forever with the Lord",
Volume 19, Sermon #1136 - Philippians 1:23

As you come nearer heaven ought you not to be more heavenly?

Forty Years,
Volume 20, Sermon #1179 - Deuteronomy 2:7

What, carry your sins into heaven? Carry hell into heaven! Man, hast thou any reason left in thee to expect God to have it so?

Reasons for Parting with Sin,
Volume 22, Sermon #1278 - Isaiah 1:18

Heaven at any price is well secured.

Our Last Journey,
Volume 23, Sermon #1373 - Job 16:22

What is heaven? It is the place which his love suggested, which his genius invented, which his bounty provided, which his royalty has adorned, which his wisdom has prepared, which he himself glorifies; in that heaven you are to be with him for ever.

"Forever with the Lord",
Volume 23, Sermon #1374 - 1 Thessalonians 4:17

"Heaven is a state," says somebody. Yes, certainly, it is a state; but it is a place too, and in the future it will be more distinctly a place.

"Let Not Your Heart Be Troubled",
Volume 29, Sermon #1741 - John 14:1-4

Above all, you must get heaven into your own heart, for you will never have your heart in heaven till you have heaven in your heart.

Abraham, a Pattern to Believers,
Volume 39, Sermon #2292 - Hebrews 11:9, 10

I do not know that in heaven they know all things—that must be for the Omniscient only—but they know all they need or really want to know; they are satisfied there.

The Bliss of the Glorified,
Volume 62, Sermon #3499 - Revelation 7:16

Hell

You and I can never imagine all the depths of hell. Shut out from us by a black veil of darkness, we cannot tell the horrors of that dismal dungeon of lost souls. Happily, the wailings of the damned have never startled us, for a thousand tempests were but a maiden's whisper, compared with one wail of a damned spirit. It is not possible for us to see the tortures of those souls who dwell eternally within an anguish that knows no alleviation. These eyes would become sightless balls of darkness, if they were permitted for an instant to look into that ghastly shrine of torment. Hell is horrible, for we may say of it, eye has not seen, nor ear heard, neither has it entered into the heart of man to conceive the horrors which God has prepared for them that hate him.

The Sympathy of Two Worlds,
Volume 4, Sermon #203 - Luke 15:10

Beloved, the eternal torment of men is no joy to God.

The Great Need-Or, the Great Salvation,
Volume 11, Sermon #610 - Isaiah 48:18

Scripture does not speak of the fire of hell as chastening and purifying, but as punishment which men shall receive for deeds done in the body. They are to be visited with many stripes, and receive just recompense for transgressions. What can there be about hell fire to change a man's heart? Surely the more the lost will suffer the more will they hate God.

Future Punishment A Fearful Thing,
Volume 12, Sermon #682 - Hebrews 10:31

If the wooings of Christ's wounds cannot make you love Christ, do you think the flames of hell will?

Future Punishment a Fearful Thing,
Volume 12, Sermon #682 - Hebrews 10:31

The doctrine of no punishment for any man is popular at this day, and threatens to have even greater sway in the future.

In Christ No Condemnation,
Volume 32, Sermon #1917 - Romans 8:1

Those who are evermore making light of hell are probably doing it in the hope of making it easy for themselves.

The Pleading of the Last Messenger,
Volume 33, Sermon #1951 - Mark 12:6-9

Hell is sin fully developed,—a man's own soul permitted to go to extreme limits with that which it now carries out in a mitigated form, and so, becoming like a furnace heated seven times hotter than usual, tormenting itself beyond all power of imagination.

God's Dealings with Eygpt and Israel,
Volume 47, Sermon #2723 - Psalm 78:51, 52

Moreover, we are persuaded that the penalties of sin will differ; and that, albeit all the wicked shall be cast into hell, yet there will be degrees in the anguish of that lost estate.

The Two Debtors,
Volume 52, Sermon #3015 - Luke 7:41, 42

It needs a whole eternity to set forth, in hell, all the justice of God in the punishment of sin.

Justice Vindicated and Righteousness Exemplified,
Volume 53, Sermon #3038 - Romans 3:24-26

Would it not be better to go to heaven side by side with a poor old almshouse-woman, or a chimney-sweep, or a pauper from the workhouse, than to go to hell with a lord, a duke, or a millionaire?

Stumbling At the Word,
Volume 57, Sermon #3258 - 1 Peter 2:8

Remember, you can be laughed into hell, but you can never be laughed out of it.

Are You Mocked?,
Volume 62, Sermon #3512 - Psalm 14:6

Holiness

What is holiness? Is it not wholeness of character? A balanced condition in which there is neither lack nor redundance.

An All Around Ministry, Page 53

It is clear that lax doctrine and lax living are pretty frequently associated.

An All Around Ministry, Page 310

Give your second best never.

An All Around Ministry, Page 393

The Christian should take nothing short of Christ for his model.

Morning and Evening, Page 161

Jesus gave both his hands to the nails, how can I keep back one of mine from His blessed work?

Morning and Evening, Page 529

There never lived a man who was too holy, and there never will live a man who will imitate Christ too closely, or avoid sin too rigidly.

We Endeavor, Page 113

I would to God that saints would cling to Christ half as earnestly as sinners cling to the devil. If we were as willing to suffer for God as some are to suffer for their lusts, what perseverance and zeal would be seen on all sides!

Kicking Against the Pricks,
Volume 12, Sermon #709 - Acts 9:5

There must be a perfect model before us before we can discern our own departures from perfection.

Heat-Knowledge of God,
Volume 20, Sermon #1206 - Jeremiah 24:7

God is making, by his grace, beings who will stand next to his throne, but will remain reverently loyal for ever.

The Three Whats,
Volume 25, Sermon #1466 - Ephesians 1:18-20

Hang that question up in your houses, "What would Jesus do?" and then think of another, "How would Jesus do it?" for what he would do, and how he would do it, may always stand as the best guide to us.

Everyday Religion,
Volume 27, Sermon #1599 - Galatians 2:20

Nearness to God brings likeness to God. The more you see God the more of God will be seen in you.

Imitators of God,
Volume 29, Sermon #1725 - Ephesians 5:1

He that has a clean heart will necessarily have clean hands.

The Singular Origin of a Christian,
Volume 31, Sermon #1829 - Ephesians 2:10

Be half a Christian, and you shall have enough religion to make you miserable; be wholly a Christian, and your joy shall be full.

The Foundation and Its Seal—A Sermon for the Times,
Volume 31, Sermon #1854 - 2 Timothy 2:19

Those whom free grace chooses, free grace cleanses. We are not chosen because we are holy, but chosen to be holy: and being chosen, the purpose is no dead letter, but we are made to seek after holiness.

The Foundation and Its Seal—A Sermon for the Times,
Volume 31, Sermon #1854 - 2 Timothy 2:19

The proof that Christ came into the world should be, that his followers are holy.

The Lord's Supper,
Volume 31, Sermon #1872 - 1 Corinthians 11:26

It often cheers my heart to think that since the Lord made me he can put me right, and keep me so to the end.

Our Own Dear Shepherd,
Volume 32, Sermon #1877 - John 10:14, 15

Godliness makes a man like God.

The form of Godliness Without the Power,
Volume 35, Sermon #2089 - 2 Timothy 3:5

Never do what you could not suppose Christ would have done.

The Rule and Reward of Serving Christ,
Volume 42, Sermon #2449 - John 12:26

If your religion does not make you holy, it will damn you as surely as you are now alive.

Learning in Private What to Teach in Public,
Volume 46, Sermon #2674 - Matthew 10:27

There are two sides to all the moral questions in the world. There is holiness, for instance. You all know on whose side that is. And there is unholiness—and you have no difficulty in deciding on whose side that is.

"Who Is on the Lord's Side?",
Volume 50, Sermon #2884 - Exodus 32:26

Aim at the highest conceivable degree of holiness; and, though you will not be perfect, never excuse yourselves because you are not.

A Blessed Gospel Chain,
Volume 50, Sermon #2895 - John 14:23

Where faith is genuine, through the Holy Spirit's power, it works a cleansing from sin, a hatred of evil, an anxious desire after holiness and it leads the soul to aspire after the image of God. Faith and holiness are inseparable.

Railings,
Volume 52, Sermon #2999 - Deuteronomy 22:8

The best service you can render to Christ is to imitate Him. If you want to do what will please Him—do as He did!

Christ's Death and Ours,
Volume 53, Sermon #3024 - John 12:23-24

Only holy Christians are useful Christians—and the preaching of Christ's Truth must be backed up by the consistent living of Christ's followers if it is to have its due effect upon the hearts and lives of the ungodly.

Pardon and Justification,
Volume 53, Sermon #3045 - Psalm 32:1

The coming of Christ into any soul, or into any church, is the death of sin and the birth of holiness!

If So—What Then?,
Volume 53, Sermon #3047 - 1 Peter 4:18

The man who is deeply discontented with himself is probably growing fast into the full likeness of Christ.

Solace for Sad Hearts,
Volume 58, Sermon #3325 - Isaiah 61:3

Holy Spirit

He suggests good thoughts, prompts good actions, reveals good truths, applies good promises, assists in good attainments, and leads to good results.

Morning and Evening, Page 95

Let me remark that being "led by the Spirit of God" is a remarkable expression. It does not say, "As many as are driven by the Spirit of God." No, the devil is a driver, and when he enters either into men or into hogs he drives them furiously.

The Leading of the Spirit, the Secret Token of the Sons of God,
Volume 21, Sermon #1220 - Romans 8:14

God, by his Spirit, brings old truth home to the heart, gives new light to our eyes, and causes the word to exercise new power over us, but he reveals no new facts, and he utters no words in any man's ears concerning his condition and state. We must be content with the old revelation and with the life and power and force with which the Holy Spirit brings it to the heart. Neither must any of us seek to have any additional revelation, for that would imply that the Scriptures are incomplete.

The True Position of the Witness Within,
Volume 24, Sermon #1428 - 1 John 5:10

The Spirit is said to do what only God can do, namely, to dwell in the hearts of all believers.

Adoption-the Spirit and the Cry,
Volume 24, Sermon #1435 - Galatians 4:6

There will never be any mighty work come from us unless there is first a mighty work in us—no man truly labors for souls unless the Holy Spirit has first worked mightily in him.

Christ the Creator,
Volume 56, Sermon #3180 - Colossians 1:16

God has been pleased to make the bodies of His people to be the temples of the Holy Spirit. At this very moment, in every one of you who have put your trust in the Lord Jesus, Deity resides!

Our Position and Our Purpose,
Volume 57, Sermon #3245 - 2 Corinthians 7:1

Though with the teaching of the Holy Spirit, every year's experience will make the Christian riper, yet without that teaching it is possible that each year may make a Christian not more ripe, but more rotten.

The Voices of Our Days,
Volume 58, Sermon #3283 - Job 32:7

It was the mighty power of the Holy Spirit dwelling in Him by which Jesus overcame the world—and that same quiet power, if it dwells in us, will make us win the same victory by faith.

Good Cheer from Christ's Victory over the World,
Volume 58, Sermon #3285 - John 16:33

Honesty

If you cannot get on honestly, be satisfied not to get on.

John Ploughman's Pictures, Page 129

Depend upon it, friends, if a straight line will not pay, a crooked one won't.

John Ploughman's Talk, Page 137

While the golden rule is more admired than practiced by ordinary men, the Christian should always do unto others as he would that they should do unto him. He should be one whose word is his bond, and who, having once pledged his word, swears to his own hurt, but changes not. There ought to be an essential difference between the Christian and the best moralist, by reason of the higher standard which the gospel inculcates, and the Savior has exemplified. Certainly, the highest point to which the best unconverted man can go might well be looked upon as a level below which the converted man will never venture to descend.

The Broad Wall,
Volume 57, Sermon #3281 - Nehemiah 3:8

Hope

Hope what you please; but remember, that hope without truth at the bottom of it, is an anchor without a holdfast. A groundless hope is a mere delusion. Christ's Incarnation, Page 146
Hell alone excepted, hope is a dweller in all regions.
The Treasury of David, Psalms 71, Verse 14

Kill hope in a man, and you have killed the man's best self.
My Own Personal Holdfast,
Volume 35, Sermon #2069 - Micah 7:7

The New Zealander has a word for hope which signifies "the swimming-thought"; because when all other thoughts are drowned, hope still swims.
Unanswered Prayer,
Volume 59, Sermon #3344 - Psalm 22:2

Humility

God comes into our heart—He finds it full—He begins to break our comforts and make it empty; then there is more room for grace. The humbler a man lies, the more comfort he will always have because he will be more fitted to receive it.
Morning and Evening, Page 86

If you seek humility, try hard work; if you would know your nothingness, attempt some great thing for Jesus.
Morning and Evening, Page 125

Have you ever noticed the difference between being humble and being humbled? Many persons are humbled who are not humble at all.
Self-Humbling,
Volume 13, Sermon #748 - 2 Chronicles 34:27

I believe every Christian man has a choice between being humble and being humbled.
Thought-Reading Extraordinary,
Volume 30, Sermon #1801 - Psalm 10:17

Humility has been rightly said to be a correct estimate of ourselves.

Christ's Motive and Ours,
Volume 37, Sermon #2232 - 2 Corinthians 8:9

Whenever you get one inch above the ground in your own esteem, you are that inch too high!

The Blessings of Public Worship,
Volume 41, Sermon #2395 - Luke 18:10

God never honors His servants with success without effectually preventing their grasping the honor of their work. If we are tempted to boast, He soon lays us low. He always whips behind the door at home those whom He most honors in public.

Railings,
Volume 52, Sermon #2999 - Deuteronomy 22:8

Growing Christians think nothing of themselves, but full-grown Christians know themselves to be less than nothing.

Jotham's Peculiar Honor,
Volume 53, Sermon #3063 - 2 Chronicles 27:6

Humor

I heard one say the other day that a certain preacher had no more gifts for the ministry than an oyster, and in my own judgment this was a slander on the oyster, for that worthy bivalve shows great discretion in his openings, and knows when to close.

An All Around Ministry, Forward!

The dreariest thing you can read is the newspaper.

Creation's Groans and the Saint's Sighs,
Volume 14, Sermon #788 - Romans 8:22, 23

Sometimes when I have said a humorous thing in preaching I have not asked you to excuse me, for if God has given me humor I mean to use it in his cause; many a man has been caught, and his ear arrested, and his attention won by a quaint remark. If any one can prove it is a wickedness, and not a natural faculty,

I will abandon it; but it is a faculty of nature, and it ought to be consecrated and used for the cause of Christ.

Redemption and Its Claims,
Volume 20, Sermon #1163 - 1 Corinthians 6:20, 1 Corinthians 7:23

There is no one part of a man's constitution, which is really a part of his manhood, which should not praise God. Ay, even the sense of humor should be sanctified to the service of the Most High!

The Keynote of the Year,
Volume 36, Sermon #2121 - Psalm 103:1

A religion that cannot stand a little laughter must be a very rotten one.

John Mark-Or, Haste in Religion,
Volume 52, Sermon #3023 - Mark 14:50-52

A man says to me, "Can you explain the seven trumpets of the Revelation?" No, but I can blow one in your ear, and warn you to escape from the wrath to come.

Enquiring the Way Zion,
Volume 53, Sermon #3035 - Jeremiah 50:5

Husbands

Happy is the man who is happy in his wife. Let him love her as he loves himself, and a little better, for she is his better half.

John Ploughman's Pictures, Page 91

He is kind to himself who is kind to his wife.

John Ploughman's Talk, Page 92

Unkind and domineering husbands ought not to pretend to be Christians, for they act clean contrary to Christ's commands.

John Ploughman's Talk, Page 92

A true wife is her husband's better half, his lump of delight, his flower of beauty, his guardian angel, and his heart's treasure.

John Ploughman's Talk, Page 120

His rib is the best bone in his body.

John Ploughman's Talk, Page 120

Women are found fault with for often looking into the glass, but that is not so bad a glass as men drown their senses in.

John Ploughman's Talk, Page 122

Say what you will of your wife's advice, it's as likely as not you will be sorry you did not take it.

John Ploughman's Talk, Page 129

Hyper Calvinism

Mark that in the father's drawing there is no compulsion whatever; Christ never compelled any man to come to him against his will. If a man be unwilling to be saved, Christ does not save him against his will.

Human Inability,
Volume 4, Sermon #182 - John 6:44

They love the doctrine of election, but there is one doctrine they love better, and that is, the doctrine of exclusion. They love to think they are shut in, but they feel quite as much delight that others are shut out.

A Secret and Yet No Secret,
Volume 8, Sermon #431 - Song of Solomon 4:12, 15.

Are there not some who think that they carry the gospel and all the doctrines of it in their pockets as if it were a five-sided lozenge? They have condensed the infinite into a pentagon.

Teaching for the Outer and Inner Circles,
Volume 28, Sermon #1669 - Mark 4:33, 34

The grace of God constrains men to become Christians, and yet only constrains them consistently with the laws of their mind. The freedom of the will is as great a truth as the predestination of God. The grace of God, without violating our wills, makes men willing in the day of God's power, and they give themselves to

Jesus Christ. You cannot be a Christian against your will. How could it be? A servant of God against his will! A child of God against his will! Nay, it never was so, and it never shall be so.

Joining the Church,
Volume 60, Sermon #3411 - 2 Corinthians 8:5

Idolatry

If you delight more in God's gifts than in God Himself, you are practically setting up another God above Him, and this you must never do.

Only a Prayer Meeting, Page 35

It is idolatry to worship the true God by a wrong method.

Tell It All,
Volume 9, Sermon #514 - Mark 5:33

No nation has ever yet risen above the character of its so-called gods.

The Gospel's Power in a Christian's Life,
Volume 11, Sermon #640 - Philippians 1:27

Whatever a man depends upon, whatever rules his mind, whatever governs his affections, whatever is the chief object of his delight, is his god.

The Root That Bears Wormwood,
Volume 12, Sermon #723 - Deuteronomy 29:18

If you love anything better than God you are idolaters: if there is anything you would not give up for God it is your idol: if there is anything that you seek with greater fervor than you seek the glory of God, that is your idol, and conversion means a turning from every idol.

A Summary of Experience and a Body of Divinity,
Volume 30, Sermon #1806 - 1 Thessalonians 1:9, 10

That is your god which rules your nature—that which is your motive power—that for which you live.

A Sweet Silver Bell Ringing in Each Believer's Heart,
Volume 31, Sermon #1819 - Micah 7:7

If you want to lose that which is the object of your comfort and delight, love it too much.

Concerning the Consolations of God,
Volume 35, Sermon #2099 - Job 15:11

A lawless man fashions for himself a lawless god.

The Father's Love His Dying Son,
Volume 35, Sermon #2117 - John 10:17

If you worship a god of gold, you will perish as much as if you worshipped a god of mud.

Three Decisive Steps,
Volume 37, Sermon #2220 - 1 Samuel 7:2-5

It is ingrained in human nature thus to seek a sign; but what is that but idolatry?

"If You Can"—"If You Can",
Volume 37, Sermon #2224 - Mark 9:22, 23

"Little children, keep yourselves from idols," was the injunction of the loving apostle John, and he wrote thus in love, because he knew that, if God sees us making idols of anything, he will either break our idols or break us.

Fifteen Years Later!,
Volume 53, Sermon #3025 - Job 1:21

Man is such an idolater that, if he cannot idolize anything else, he will idolize himself, and set himself up, and bow down and worship himself.

Love and Jealousy,
Volume 62, Sermon #3516 - Song of Solomon 8:6

Impatience

A hasty man never is a wise man.

A Visit the Harvest Field,
Volume 17, Sermon #1025 - James 5:7, 8

It is wonderful how amiable we all are until we are irritated.

The King's Weighings,
Volume 29, Sermon #1736 - 1 Samuel 2:3

We are all impatient as long as we are imperfect. It is the mark of the child that he is in a violent hurry where men are steady.

Renewing Strength,
Volume 29, Sermon #1756 - Isaiah 40:31

We are some of us too much in a hurry to go fast. If we were a little slower, we should be quicker.

A Gracious Dismissal,
Volume 37, Sermon #2183 - Luke 7:50

Jesus Christ

He entered into all that men did except their sins.

A Good Start, Page 21

the Lord Jesus Christ acted in what He did as a great public representative person, and His dying upon the cross was the virtual dying of all His people.

Morning and Evening, Page 669

Having made Jesus his all, he shall find all in Jesus.

Morning and Evening, Page 705

Either He bore all our sins, or none; and He either saves us once for all, or not at all.

The Soul Winner, Page 20

God's Anointed is appointed, and shall not be disappointed.

The Treasury of David, Psalm 2, Verse 6

Trust Christ, but do not trust yourself.

Jacob and Esau,
Volume 5, Sermon #239 - Romans 9:13

He will reign over you, either by your consent, or without it.

Good News for Loyal Subjects,
Volume 14, Sermon #807 - 1 Corinthians 15:25

God has such affection for our race that he has married our nature to himself.

The Parable of the Wedding Feast,
Volume 17, Sermon #975 - Matthew 22:2, 3, 4

See how low he fell to lift us from our fall!

The Crown of Thorns,
Volume 20, Sermon #1168 - Matthew 27:29

The blood of Christ is still on the earth, for when Jesus bled it fell upon the ground and was never gathered up.

The Three Witnesses,
Volume 20, Sermon #1187 - 1 John 5:8

Those who deny the Godhead of Christ are consistent in rejecting the atonement.

Jesus, the Substitute for His People,
Volume 21, Sermon #1223 - Romans 8:34

Depend upon it, my hearer, you never will go to heaven unless you are prepared to worship Jesus Christ as God.

Jesus, the Delight of Heaven,
Volume 21, Sermon #1225 - Revelation 5:9, 10

A bloodless gospel is a lifeless gospel; if the atonement be denied or frittered away, or put into a secondary place, or obscured, in that proportion the life has gone out of the religion which is professed.

The Sacred Love-Token,
Volume 21, Sermon #1251 - Exodus 12:13

He was a man of sorrows, but he was not a preacher of sorrows, neither do his life or his discourses leave an unhappy impression upon the mind.

The Oil of Gladness,
Volume 22, Sermon #1273 - Psalm 45:7

Why was the fountain filled with blood if you need no washing? Is Christ a superfluity? Oh, it cannot be.

Christ the End of Law,
Volume 22, Sermon #1325 - Romans 10:4

God in the carpenter's shop! The Son of God driving nails and handling a hammer! Wondrous work, this!

The Student's Prayer,
Volume 23, Sermon #1344 - Psalm 119:27

We write Jesus' name upon our banner, for it is hell's terror, heaven's delight and earth's hope.

Jesus Christ Himself,
Volume 23, Sermon #1388 - Ephesians 2:20

Jesus Christ himself is to us precept, for he is the way: he is to us doctrine, for he is the truth: he is to us experience, for he is the life.

Jesus Christ Himself,
Volume 23, Sermon #1388 - Ephesians 2:20

When God laid sin upon Christ it must have been in the intent of his heart that he would never lay it on those for whom Christ died.

Peace—A Fact and a Feeling,
Volume 25, Sermon #1456 - Romans 5:1

All historians must confess that the turning point of the race is the cross of Christ. It would be impossible to fix any other hinge of history. From that moment the power of evil received its mortal wound.

The Holy Spirit's Threefold Conviction of Men,
Volume 29, Sermon #1708 - John 16:8-11

He who can do all things without Christ will end in doing nothing.

On Humbling Ourselves Before God,
Volume 29, Sermon #1733 - 1 Peter 5:6

He that made man was made man.

Our Sympathizing High Priest,
Volume 32, Sermon #1927 - Hebrews 5:7-10

"I came, I saw, I conquered," is a line which will be quoted to the end of time. Such is the life of our Lord Jesus, from the cross onward.

Our Ascended Lord,
Volume 32, Sermon #1928 - 1 Peter 3:22

I wish that our ministry—that mine especially—might be tied and tethered to the cross. I have no other subject to set before you but Jesus only.

The Best Bread,
Volume 33, Sermon #1940 - John 6:48

He is not a deified man anymore than He is a humanized God.

The Lord's Own View of His Church and People,
Volume 33, Sermon #1957 - Song of Solomon 4:12

Leave out the cross, and you have killed the religion of Jesus. Atonement by the blood of Jesus is not an arm of Christian truth; it is the heart of it.

The Blood Shed of Many,
Volume 33, Sermon #1971 - Matthew 26:28

The first Adam came to the fig tree for leaves, but the Second Adam looks for figs.

The Withered Fig Tree,
Volume 35, Sermon #2107 - Matthew 21:17-20

With a Savior less than divine you have a religion less than saving.

The Question of Questions,
Volume 36, Sermon #2141 - John 9:35

He comes to us in two ways—in his human nature, born; in his divine nature, given.

Immanuel—The Light of Life,
Volume 36, Sermon #2163 - Isaiah 9:1, 2

Beloved, there is a cure for every spiritual disease in the cross.

Our Lord in the Valley of Humiliation,
Volume 38, Sermon #2281 - Philippians 2:8

He did not die to make men salvable; he died to save them.

Christ's One Sacrifice for Sin,
Volume 38, Sermon #2283 - Hebrews 9:26

Some people like laziness; Christ loved activity.

The Lord's Chosen Ministers,
Volume 39, Sermon #2319 - Luke 10:21

Christ as bread, yet not eaten, becomes Christ dishonored.

"Take, Eat",
Volume 40, Sermon #2350 - Matthew 26:26

Think not of the sinner, or of the greatness of his sin, but think of the greatness of the Savior!

"A Man Under Authority",
Volume 41, Sermon #2434 - Matthew 8:8, 9

If we are ever ashamed of loving Christ, we have good reason to be ashamed of such shameful shame!

Christ's Perfection and Precedence,
Volume 42, Sermon #2478 - Song of Solomon 5:10

Christ on the Cross saves us when He becomes to us Christ in the heart.

Christ's Perfection and Precedence,
Volume 42, Sermon #2478 - Song of Solomon 5:10

There are no good works except those that spring from a living, loving, lasting faith in God through Jesus Christ our Lord!

How Please God,
Volume 43, Sermon #2513 - Hebrews 11:6

Oh, I never imagined how strong Christ was till I saw His love hold back His Deity!

Jesus Sitting On the Well,
Volume 44, Sermon #2570 - John 4:6

You have never truly found Jesus if you do not tell others about Him!

The Baptist's Message,
Volume 45, Sermon #2646 - John 1:29

Ah, Lord Jesus! I never knew Your love till I understood the meaning of Your death.

The Death of Christ for His People,
Volume 46, Sermon #2656

"Do you believe?" said the Lord Jesus to this man, and by that question He held him fast. That is the way to win souls, begin with a personal question!

A Pressed Man Yielding Christ,
Volume 46, Sermon #2667 - John 9:35-38

Whenever there is a cross to be carried by any of Christ's followers, He always bears the heavy end on His own shoulders.

Our Hiding Place,
Volume 49, Sermon #2856 - Isaiah 32:2

How can we remember his death without sorrowing over the sin which made that death necessary?

Christ's Crowning Glory,
Volume 50, Sermon #2876 - Psalm 21:5

God made the world without any suffering, but he could not redeem even one soul without agonies unknown.

New Tokens of Ancient Love,
Volume 50, Sermon #2880 - Jeremiah 31:3

There is no cure for the love of sin like the blood of Christ!

A Dire Disease Strangely Cured,
Volume 50, Sermon #2887 - Isaiah 53:5, 1 Peter 2:24

A religion without the blood of Christ in it is a lifeless religion. A religion without the Atonement and reconciliation by the blood of the Covenant has missed the most essential part of true godliness!

Sham Conversion,
Volume 51, Sermon #2928 - 2 Kings 17:25, 33, 34

Everything that has to do with Christ's work is of real, practical, vital consequence to Believers. He is to be the food for our souls.

Faith is to receive Him. Love is to embrace Him. Hope is to rejoice in Him!

Too Little for the Lamb,
Volume 51, Sermon #2937 - Exodus 12:3, 4

We all know what our own cross is. And if our Heavenly Father has appointed it for us, we must take it up and follow Christ!

A Procession of Cross-Bearers,
Volume 51, Sermon #2946 - Mark 10:21

When a man has no self remaining, but has given himself up as a living sacrifice for Christ, that which would be a terror to another man becomes a comfort to him.

The Church—The World's Hope,
Volume 51, Sermon #2952

It has been often said that there are but two steps to Heaven—and that those two are but one—out of self and into Christ.

The Big Gates Wide Open,
Volume 51, Sermon #2954 - John 6:37

Christ, my Brothers and Sisters, is the point of union for all the soldiers of the Cross.

Our Banner,
Volume 52, Sermon #2979 - Psalm 60:4

I do not care to what church you belong, or what creed you are ready to die for, you do not know the Truth of God unless the Person of Christ is dear to you!

A Sermon from a Sick Preacher,
Volume 52, Sermon #3014 - 1 Peter 2:7

Self and the Savior can never live in one heart. He will have all, or none. So, where self is on the throne, it cannot be expected that Christ should meekly come and sit upon the footstool.

Why Christ Is Not Esteemed,
Volume 53, Sermon #3033 - Isaiah 53:3

He that believes in Jesus is safe forever!

The Sparrow and the Swallow,
Volume 53, Sermon #3041 - Psalm 84:3

There is room in Christ's heart for all who come to Him, so let many come now.

Lessons from a Dovecot,
Volume 53, Sermon #3051 - Isaiah 60:8

It is easy to get black by sin, but remember that it is so hard to get clean that only God's Omnipotence, in the Person of Christ, could provide a Cleanser for your sins.

The Guilt and the Cleansing,
Volume 53, Sermon #3056 - Psalm 51:7

Christ came to bring healing to those who are spiritually sick—you say that you are perfectly well, so you must go your own way and Christ will go in another direction—towards sinners.

The Poor Man's Friend,
Volume 53, Sermon #3059 - Psalm 10:14

The reason for pardon is not in the penitent, but in the Pardoner.

Unknown Depths and Heights,
Volume 53, Sermon #3068 - Luke 23:34

Now, remember, you will never know the fulness of Christ until you know the emptiness of everything else but Christ.

Thrice Happy Day!,
Volume 54, Sermon #3073 - Haggai 2:19

The more I consider the doctrine of substitution, the more is my soul enamored of the matchless wisdom of God which devised this system of salvation. As for a hazy atonement which atones for everybody in general, and for nobody in particular,—an atonement made equally for Judas and for John, I care nothing for it; but a literal, substitutionary sacrifice, Christ vicariously bearing the wrath of God on my behalf, this calms my conscience with regard to the righteous demands of the law of God, and satisfies the instincts of my nature which declare that, as God is just, he must exact the penalty of my guilt.

"Marvelous Things",
Volume 54, Sermon #3086 - Psalm 98:1, 2

The life of Christ is in you by reason of His death. for you the Holy Spirit has so worked in you that the life of God is within you and you can never die! Because Christ lives, you must also live.

Knowing and Doing,
Volume 54, Sermon #3092 - 2 Corinthians 8:9

Oh, it is a blessed thing to feel that you are living, not as a servant of man, nor of the Church, nor of a sect, or party, but of Him whose precious blood has bought you!

Concentration and Diffusion,
Volume 55, Sermon #3174 - John 12:3

When Jesus said, "I am the Way," He clearly intended to exclude all other ways, so beware lest you perish in any one of them!

The Last Message for the Year,
Volume 56, Sermon #3230 - John 6:37

He became man out of love to men.

Pleading with the Indifferent,
Volume 59, Sermon #3360 - Lamentations 1:12

If Christ is not first with you, Christ is nothing to you.

"Christ Is All",
Volume 61, Sermon #3446 - Colossians 3:11

Joy

There is no monotony in real joy.

Barbed Arrows, Page 281

Our hope in Christ for the future is the mainspring and the mainstay of our joy here.

Morning and Evening, Page 552

There are ten thousand arguments in Scripture for happiness in the Christian; but I do not know that there is one logical argument for misery.

Our Stronghold,
Volume 9, Sermon #491 - Proverbs 18:10

The chief joy of life is to be right with yourself, your neighbor, your God.

The Exeter-Hall Sermon Young Men,
Volume 29, Sermon #1740 - Psalm 116:16

Happy religion in which it is our duty to be glad!

"Let Not Your Heart Be Troubled",
Volume 29, Sermon #1741 - John 14:1-4

Our greatest joys swim on the crests of the huge billows of trouble.

A Delicious Experience,
Volume 35, Sermon #2090 - Hebrews 4:3

We have never had anything from our Master but it has ultimately tended to our joy.

A Harp of Ten Strings,
Volume 37, Sermon #2219 - Luke 1:46, 47

You may judge a man by his joy; as a man rejoices, so is he.

The Lord's Chosen Ministers,
Volume 39, Sermon #2319 - Luke 10:21

It is not so much what I have as what I shall have that makes me joyful.

The Hope That Purifies,
Volume 57, Sermon #3235 - 1 John 3:3

We have seen men with money, who were not happy; we have seen men with honor, who were not happy; we have seen persons in power, with the command of empires, who were not happy; but we never saw, and never shall see, the individual who has Jesus with him, that is not happy.

A Present Helper,
Volume 61, Sermon #3447 - Acts 18:10

Justification

Sometimes we cannot see the light, but God always sees the light, and that is much better than our seeing it. Better for the judge to see my innocence than for me to think I see it.

Morning and Evening, Page 11

Are they who stand before the throne of God justified now?—so are we, as truly and as clearly justified as they who walk in white and sing melodious praises to celestial harps.

Morning and Evening, Page 272

We shall grow in grace, but we shall never be more completely pardoned than when we first believed: we shall one day stand before the glorious presence of God in his own sacred courts, and see the Well-beloved and wear his likeness, but we shall not even then be more perfectly forgiven than we are at this present moment.

The First Note of My Song,
Volume 25, Sermon #1492 - Psalm 103:3

Alas, I may be sinning, for even in the holiest deeds we do there is still sin, but even then God is still forgiving. If indeed you are a believer in Jesus Christ the Lord is at all times forgiving you: as constant as your sin so constant is his forgiveness.

The First Note of My Song,
Volume 25, Sermon #1492 - Psalm 103:3

You are often sinning, but he is always forgiving you; you are often wandering, often erring, often grieving him, but "he forgiveth all thine iniquities." I do not feel like preaching when I touch this text. I heartily wish I could sit down and have a happy cry over this blessed truth that my God is at this moment forgiving me.

The First Note of My Song,
Volume 25, Sermon #1492 - Psalm 103:3

Knowledge

The knowledge of our ignorance is the doorstep of the temple of knowledge.

Christ's Incarnation, Page 98

A very small book would hold most men's learning, and every line would have a mistake in it.

John Ploughman's Pictures, Page 142

An ounce of heart knowledge is worth a ton of head learning.

Morning and Evening, Page 576

What we know is as nothing when compared with what we know not.

Sin Immeasurable,
Volume 6, Sermon #299 - Psalm 19:12

The usual rule is that the more we really know the more conscious we are of the littleness of our knowledge.

Sins of Ignorance,
Volume 23, Sermon #1386 - Leviticus 5:17, 18

If knowledge were bliss the devil would be in heaven.

A Discourse Upon True Blessedness Here and Hereafter,
Volume 31, Sermon #1874 - James 1:12

There are two great certainties about things that shall come to pass—one is that God knows, and the other is that we do not know.

God's Will About the Future,
Volume 38, Sermon #2242 - James 4:13-17

Now, remember, you will never know the fullness of Christ until you know the emptiness of everything else but Christ!

Thrice Happy Day!,
Volume 54, Sermon #3073 - Haggai 2:19

Observe, then, that all other knowledge may be useful enough in itself, but if it does not concern Christ, it cannot be called saving knowledge.

Knowing and Believing,
Volume 58, Sermon #3331 - 2 Timothy 1:12

It is not enough to know about Christ, it is knowing Christ Himself that alone saves the soul!

Knowing and Believing,
Volume 58, Sermon #3331 - 2 Timothy 1:12

You know something of Him. Oh, may God give the Grace to add to your knowledge, trust, and then shall you have true saving faith!

Knowing and Believing,
Volume 58, Sermon #3331 - 2 Timothy 1:12

I should not like to say a hard thing of God's people, but I believe there are many of them who do not want to know too much.

The Great Teacher and Remembrancer,
Volume 59, Sermon #3353 - John 14:26

Law

Once more: the entrance of the law makes the offense to abound in this sense, that the rebellious will of man rises up in opposition to it. Because God commands, man refuses; and because he forbids, man desires.

Grace Abounding Over Abounding Sin,
Volume 34, Sermon #2012 - Romans 5:20

Depend upon it, there is nothing wrong but the law condemns it, and there is nothing right but the law approves it.

The Law's Failure and Fulfillment,
Volume 37, Sermon #2228 - Romans 8:3, 4

There is nothing in the law of God that will rob you of happiness; it only denies you that which would cost you sorrow.

Repentance After Conversion,
Volume 41, Sermon #2419 - Psalm 51:17

Even Moses could not carry those tables in his hand without breaking them, nor can I do any better than he did.

God's Writing Upon Man's Heart,
Volume 52, Sermon #2992 - Jeremiah 31:33

The law is such a law that Adam failed to keep it, though innocent; how, then, shall you keep it while imperfect?

Life's Inevitable Burden,
Volume 59, Sermon #3355 - Galatians 6:6

Laziness

The men who escape without abuse in this world are the men who do nothing at all.

Words of Wisdom, Page 105

The sin of doing nothing is about the biggest of all sins, for it involves most of the others.

Words of Wisdom, Page 136

Alas, the loiterers are many, but the laborers are few.

Farm Laborers,
Volume 27, Sermon #1602 - 1 Corinthians 3:6-9

He who does little dreams much.

One Lion, Two Lions, No Lion At All!,
Volume 28, Sermon #1670 - Proverbs 26:13, 22:13

If you are idle in Christ's work, you are active in the devil's work.

The Sluggard's Farm,
Volume 34, Sermon #2027 - Proverbs 24:30-32

The Book of Proverbs deals very hard blows against sluggards, and Christian ministers do well frequently to denounce the great sin of idleness, which is the mother of a huge family of sins.

The Commissariat of the Universe,
Volume 55, Sermon #3149 - Psalm 104:28

Idle Christians are often unhappy Christians.

The Bliss of the Glorified,
Volume 62, Sermon #3499 - Revelation 7:16

Leadership

While Committees waste their time over resolutions, do

something. While Societies and Unions are making constitutions, let us win souls. Too often we discuss, and discuss, and discuss, while Satan only laughs in his sleeve. It is time we had done planning, and sought something to plan.

An All Around Ministry, Page 55

One marvels at the little things over which an assembly will waste hours of precious time, contending as if the destiny of the whole world and the fate of the starry heavens depended upon the debate.

An All Around Ministry, Page 190

To have a great many aims and objects is much the same thing as having no aim at all; for if a man shoots at many things he will hit none, or none worth the hitting.

A Good Start, Page 303

A wise man does at first what a fool does at last.

John Ploughman's Pictures, Page 20

Very little is done right when it is left to other people.

John Ploughman's Pictures, Page 124

A world where everything was easy would be a nursery for babies, but not at all a fit place for men.

John Ploughman's Pictures, Page 127

All human work which does not begin and end in the Lord Jesus must be a non-success.

Labor in Vain,
Volume 10, Sermon #567 - Jonah 1:12, 13

Those who do much already, are usually the people who can do more.

More and More,
Volume 17, Sermon #998 - Psalm 71:14

All talk influences more or less.

The Talking Book,
Volume 17, Sermon #1017 - Proverbs 6:22

We must be all conscious that we imitate those whom we admire. Love has a strange influence over our nature, to mould it into the form beloved.

The Choice of A Leader,
Volume 21, Sermon #1248 - Luke 6:39, 40

Always have something in hand that is greater than your present capacity.

The Necessity of Growing Faith,
Volume 31, Sermon #1857 - 2 Thessalonians 1:3

Well, dear friend, it goes without saying that if you managed things, they would be managed perfectly; but, you see, you cannot do everything, and therefore you must trust somebody.

Sowing in the Wind, Reaping Under Clouds,
Volume 38, Sermon #2264 - Ecclesiastes 11:4

Wellington used to say that no man is fit to command until he has learned to obey; and I am sure that it is so.

Obeying Christ's Orders,
Volume 39, Sermon #2317 - John 2:5

It is no use having a brain that is taken up with fifty different subjects, and yet does not master any one of them.

Girded for the Work,
Volume 45, Sermon #2649 - 1 Peter 1:13

Do you not also know that the way to be really great is to be little, and that he who is greatest of all is the one who has learned to be least of all?

Anxiety, Ambition, Indecision,
Volume 50, Sermon #2871 - Luke 12:29

Nothing good will be done by a man who will not attempt it until everybody thinks it is wise.

God-Guided Men,
Volume 54, Sermon #3078 - Galatians 1:16

Lost

For a little sin, or for a sin, however great, which had but little of evil in its consequences, we might have been saved by some finite being; but if God himself must quit his high abode, and sojourn here to be our Savior, then was our ruin terrible in the extreme.

Adorning the Gospel,
Volume 41, Sermon #2416 - Titus 2:10

It is a dreadful thing for anyone to be lost; I do not know if there is a more dreadful word in the English language than that word "lost."

Why the Gospel Is Hidden,
Volume 58, Sermon #3288 - 2 Corinthians 4:3

They are so lost that they need saving, but they are also so lost that they need seeking.

Christ the Seeker and Savior of the Lost,
Volume 58, Sermon #3309 - Luke 19:10

What is meant by "the lost"? Well, "lost" is a dreadful word. I should need much time to explain it; but if the Spirit of God, like a flash of light, shall enter into your heart, and show you what you are by nature, you will accept that word "lost" as descriptive of your condition, and understand it better than a thousand words of mine could enable you to do. Lost by the fall; lost by inheriting a depraved nature; lost by your own acts and deeds; lost by a thousand omissions of duty, and lost by countless deeds of overt transgression; lost by habits of sin; lost by tendencies and inclinations which have gathered strength and dragged you downward into deeper and yet deeper darkness and iniquity; lost by inclinations which never turn of themselves to that which is right, but which resolutely refuse divine mercy and infinite love. We are lost willfully and willingly; lost perversely and utterly; but still lost of our own accord, which is the worst kind of being lost that possibly can be. We are lost to God, who has lost our heart's love, and lost our confidence, and lost our obedience; lost to the church, which we cannot serve; lost to truth, which we will not see; lost to right, which cause we do not uphold; lost to heaven, into whose sacred precincts we can never come; lost—so lost that unless almighty mercy shall intervene, we shall be cast into the pit that is bottomless to sink for ever. "LOST! LOST! LOST!" the very word seems to me to be the knell of an impenitent soul. "Lost! Lost! Lost!" I hear the dismal tolling! A soul's funeral is being celebrated. Endless death has befallen an immortal being! It comes up as a dreadful wail from far beyond the boundaries of life and hope, forth from those dreary regions of death and darkness where spirits dwell who would not have Christ to reign over them. "Lost! Lost! Lost!" Ah me, that ever these ears should hear that doleful sound! Better a whole world on fire than a single soul lost! Better every star quenched and yon skies a wreck than a single soul to be lost!

Christ the Seeker and Savior of the Lost,
Volume 58, Sermon #3309 - Luke 19:10

Love

Nothing gives Christ greater delight than the love of His people.

A Good Start, Page 200

We shall not long have love to man if we do not first and chiefly cultivate love to God.

A Good Start, Page 314

Your Lord is very jealous of your love, O believer. Did He choose you? He cannot bear that you should choose another.

Morning and Evening, Page 512

Love not clay as if it were undying—love not dust as though it were eternal.

The Wailing of Risca,
Volume 7, Sermon #349 - Jeremiah 4:20

You are no lover of Christ if you do not love his children. As soon as ever the heart is given to the master of the house it is given to the children of the house. Love Christ and you will soon love all that love him.

The Queen of the South, Or the Earnest Enquirer,
Volume 9, Sermon #533 - Matthew 12:42

I could not help saying once, I remember, that I would love God even if he damned me, because he was so gracious to others.

Ben-Hadad's Escape—An Encouragement for Sinner,
Volume 9, Sermon #535 - 1 Kings 20:31-34

We are sure he loves who dies for love.

Love's Crowning Deed,
Volume 19, Sermon #1128 - John 15:13

You cannot love a thing without becoming something like it, in proportion to the force of love; and just in proportion as you love Jesus you must get like him.

An Objection and An Answer,
Volume 22, Sermon #1280 - Galatians 5:6

That love which would lead its beloved into sin is lust; it deserves not the name of love; but true love will ever seek the highest health and wholeness (which is holiness) of its object. Pure affection will grieve to see a fault, mourn over a folly, and seek to remove a blot. Perfect love seeks the perfection of the thing it loves.

The Sitting of the Refiner,
Volume 27, Sermon #1575 - Malachi 3:3

Perhaps some of you do not feel that there is anything very remarkable in this love of the Lord to the loveless. I should like you to try if you could love somebody who has nothing about him that is at all lovable.

Love's Climax,
Volume 41, Sermon #2394, 1 John 4:10

Christians, you are to love one another, not because of the gain which you get from one another, but rather because of the good you can do to one another.

Christ's "New Commandment",
Volume 51, Sermon #2936 - John 13:34, 35

Love cannot endure a doubt. If love is crossed with doubt it becomes jealousy, and that is cruel as the grave.

Positivism,
Volume 55, Sermon #3161 - 1 John 5:18-20

Love is the chief endowment for a pastor. You must love Christ if you mean to serve Him in the capacity of pastors.

"Feed My Sheep",
Volume 56, Sermon #3211 - John 21:16

Love to Him will breed a love for all His sheep and your love for them will give you power over them.

"Feed My Sheep",
Volume 56, Sermon #3211 - John 21:16

Lukewarm Religion

Philip Henry's advice to his daughter: "If you would keep warm in this cold season (January, 1692), take these four directions: 1. Get into the sun; under his blessed beams there are warmth and comfort. 2. Go near the fire. "Is not my word like a fire?" How many cheering passages are there! 3. Keep in motion and action—stirring up the grace and gift of God that is in you. 4. Seek Christian communion. "How can one be warm alone?""

Feathers for Arrows, Page 237

It is the loss of your first love that makes you seek the comfort of your bodies instead of the prosperity of your souls.

Declension from First Love,
Volume 4, Sermon #217 - Revelation 2:4

Religion cannot long be lukewarm; it will either die out or it will kindle and set you all on fire.

With the King for His Work!,
Volume 24, Sermon #1400 - 1 Chronicles 4:23

Everywhere, lukewarmness in religion is to be loathed and abandoned, for it is a gross and glaring inconsistency!

Lukewarmness,
Volume 48, Sermon #2802 - Revelation 3:15, 16

I believe that many professing Christians are cold and uncomfortable because they are doing nothing for their Lord; but if they actively served him, their blood would begin to circulate spiritually, and it would be well with them.

Lessons from the Malta Fire,
Volume 55, Sermon #3136 - Acts 28:2

Lying

He who tells little lies, will soon think nothing of great ones, for the principle is the same.

John Ploughman's Talk, Page 155

When we begin to be believers we cease to be liars.

Guile Forsaken When Guilt Is forgiven,
Volume 23, Sermon #1346 - Psalm 32:2

I have heard of men who mark a hundred as a hundred and twenty, and who mark goods as of certain lengths when they know they are not of such lengths; and they say, "It is the custom of the trade." Well, if it be the custom of your trade to lie, remember that it is God's custom to send all liars to hell.

The Lower Courts,
Volume 55, Sermon #3152 - 1 John 3:20, 21

Liars have need of good memories.

Two Coverings and Two Consequences,
Volume 62, Sermon #3500 - Proverbs 38:13, Psalm 85:2

Marriage

You expect that you will be married, and then your troubles will be over; some say that then they begin. I do not endorse that statement; but I am sure that they are not over, for there is another set of trials that begin then.

A Good Start, Page 57

It is wise to marry when we can marry wisely, and then the sooner the better.

John Ploughman's Pictures, Page 87

Married life is not all sugar, but grace in the heart will keep away most of the sours.

John Ploughman's Pictures, Page 92

When husbands and wives are well yoked, how light their load becomes!

John Ploughman's Pictures, Page 92

I have no doubt that where there is much love there will be much to love, and where love is scant faults will be plentiful.

John Ploughman's Pictures, Page 127

A life of misery is usually the lot of those who are united in marriage, or in any other way of their own choosing, with the men of the world.

Morning and Evening, Page 26

When men and women are about to be married how much of life then trembles in the balances! Upon the choice of a partner in life the fashion of that life may depend. Whether self or Christ, the world or God, shall be the master-motive of the household, may be decided by the finger which wears the plain gold ring.

The Inner Side of Conversion,
Volume 35, Sermon #2104 - Jeremiah 31:18-20

Marriage was the last relic of paradise left among men, and Jesus hasted to honor it with his first miracle.

The Beginning of Miracles Which Jesus Did,
Volume 36, Sermon #2155

Mercy

There is no greater mercy that I know of on earth than good health except it is sickness—and that has often been a greater mercy to me than health.

Christ the Cure for the Troubled Hearts,
Volume 41, Sermon #2408 - Luke 24:38

Missions

We must have the heathen converted; God has myriads of His elect among them, we must go and search for them somehow or other.

An All Around Ministry, Page 56

One of the great Missionary Societies actually informs us, by one of its writers, that it does not send out missionaries to save the heathen from the wrath to come, but to prepare them "for the higher realm which awaits them beyond the river of death." I confess that I have better hopes for the future of the heathen than for the state of those who thus write concerning them.

Only a Prayer Meeting, Page 14

The surest way to promote godliness abroad is to labour for it at home.

Only a Prayer Meeting, Page 17

In many ways the great Head of the Church scatters His servants abroad; but they ought of themselves to scatter voluntarily. Every Christian should say, "Where can I do the most good?" and if he can do more good anywhere beneath the sun than in the land of his birth, he is bound to go there, if he can. God will have us scattered; and if we will not go afield willingly, He may use providential necessity as the forcible means of our dispersion.

We Endeavor, Page 134

You will never make a missionary of the person who does no good at home.

We Endeavor, Page 139

Ah! if we did but love Christ better, my brothers and sisters, if we lived nearer to the cross, if we knew more of the value of his blood, if we wept like him over Jerusalem, if we felt more what it was for souls to perish, and what it was for men to be saved—if we did but rejoice with Christ in the prospect of his seeing the travail of his soul, and being abundantly satisfied—if we did but delight more in the divine decree, that the kingdoms of this world shall be given to Christ, I am sure we would all of us find more ways and more means for sending forth the gospel of Christ.

The Desolations of the Lord—The Consolations of His Saints,
Volume 4, Sermon #190 - Psalm 46:8, 9

I solemnly feel that my position in England will not permit my leaving the sphere in which I now am, or else to-morrow I would offer myself as a missionary.

The Missionaries' Charge and Charter,
Volume 7, Sermon #383 - Matthew 28:18, 19

If there be any one point in which the Christian church ought to keep its fervor at a white heat, it is concerning missions to the heathens. If there be anything about which we cannot tolerate lukewarmness, it is in the matter of sending the gospel to a dying world.

A Young Man's Vision,
Volume 14, Sermon #806 - Acts 2:17

The human mind is the same everywhere. Its sins may take another form, but there are just the same difficulties in one place as in another.

A Young Man's Vision,
Volume 14, Sermon #806 - Acts 2:17

The missionary enterprise, apart from supernatural influences, is the most insane that ever crossed the mind of man. Yea, I will venture to say, that the work of preaching the gospel, even in Christian England, is of all attempts the most foolish, unless we believe in the celestial power, which alone can make preaching to be of any avail.

The Pleiades and Orion,
Volume 14, Sermon #818 - Job 38:31

There is a prayer I mean to continue to offer until it is answered, that God would pour out on this church a missionary spirit. I want to see our young men devoting themselves to the work, some that will not be afraid to venture and preach Jesus Christ in the regions beyond.

Marah, Or the Bitter Waters Sweetened,
Volume 17, Sermon #987 - Exodus 15:23, 24, 25

By the love and wounds and death of Christ, by your own salvation, by your indebtedness to Jesus, by the terrible condition of the heathen, and by that awful hell whose yawning mouth is before them, ought you not to say, "Here am I; send me"?

The Divine Call for Missionaries,
Volume 23, Sermon #1351 - Isaiah 6:8

We tell our young men in the College that they must prove that they have not to go, or else their duty is clear. If some of the men of Israel had said to Joshua, "We cannot go to Ai," Joshua would have replied, "You must prove that you cannot go or you may not be excused." All other things being equal ministers should take it for granted that it is their duty to invade new territory unless they can prove to the contrary.

All the People at Work for Jesus,
Volume 23, Sermon #1358

We best promote the interests of nations when we advance the cause of God.

On Whose Side Are You?,
Volume 26, Sermon #1531 - Exodus 36:26

He that will not serve the Lord in the Sunday-school at home, will not win children to Christ in China. Distance lends no real enchantment to Christian service.

All At It,
Volume 34, Sermon #2044 - Acts 8:4, 5, Acts 8:35

As we should have no horticulture if men had no gardens, so we shall have no missionary work done unless each person has a mission.

The Mustard Seed—A Sermon for the Sunday School Teacher,
Volume 35, Sermon #2110 - Luke 13:18-19

Look at the myriads of Africa, and the millions in China and India, who have never heard the gospel. I leave their future in the hands of God all-merciful; but they cannot enter heaven.

Number 2400-Or, "Escape for Your Life!",
Volume 41, Sermon #2400 - Genesis 19:17

He who does not serve God where he is would not serve God anywhere else.

Saying Versus Doing,
Volume 47, Sermon #2747 - Matthew 21:28-30

I remember one who spoke on the missionary question one day saying, "The great question is not 'Will not the heathen be saved if we do not send them the gospel?' but 'Are we saved ourselves if we do not send them the gospel?'"

Facing the Wind,
Volume 51, Sermon #2918 - 2 Thessalonians 3:13

The Bible is not the light of the world, it is the light of the Church. But the world does not read the Bible, the world reads Christians! "You are the light of the world."

Cleansing—Wrong or Right?,
Volume 53, Sermon #3069 - John 9:30, 31

Every Christian here is either a missionary or an impostor.

A Sermon and a Reminiscence,
Volume 54, Sermon #3112 - 1 Peter 2:7

It is an honor to be allowed to serve Christ, but God will bestow still further honor upon those who faithfully serve Him!

Good Cheer from Christ's Victory over the World,
Volume 58, Sermon #3285 - John 16:33

The joy in harvest rightly consists in part in the reward of earnest labor—may such be the joy we find in serving our Lord!

Joy in Harvest,
Volume 58, Sermon #3315 - Isaiah 9:3

Mormonism

I have sometimes heard of the "Latter Day Saints." I do not know much about them, but I greatly prefer the "Every Day Saints." Those people who are saints anywhere and everywhere are truly saints; and he that is not a saint everywhere is not a saint anywhere, for this is a thing that cannot be put off and on like our Sunday dress.

Concerning Saints,
Volume 30, Sermon #1796 - Psalm 145:10

One of the most modern pretenders to inspiration is the Book of Mormon. I could not blame you should you laugh outright while I read aloud a page from that farrago.

Our Manifesto,
Volume 37, Sermon #2185 - Galatians 1:11

Mothers

O dear mothers, you have a very sacred trust reposed in you by God! He has in effect said to you, "Take this child and nurse it for Me, and I will give thee thy wages." You are called to equip the future man of God, that he may be thoroughly furnished unto every good work. If God spares you, you may live to hear that pretty boy speak to thousands, and you will have the sweet reflection in your heart that the quiet teachings of the nursery led the man to love his God and serve Him. Those who think that a woman detained at home by her little family is doing nothing, think the reverse of what is true. Scarcely can the godly mother quit her home for a place of worship; but dream not that she is lost to the work of the church; far from it, she is doing the best possible service for her Lord. Mothers, the godly training of your offspring is your first and most pressing duty.

Come Ye Children, Page 112

There is never a babe dropped into a mother's bosom but it brings care, labour, grief, and anxiety with it.

An Anxious Enquiry for A Beloved Son,
Volume 24, Sermon #1433 - 2 Samuel 18:29

Our fathers are all very well—God bless them!—and a father's godly influence and earnest prayers are of untold value to his children; but the mothers are worth two of them, mostly, as to the moral training and religious bent of their sons and daughters.

Young Man! A Prayer for You,
Volume 37, Sermon #2215 - 2 Kings 6:17

There is, somehow, a wonderful power about a mother's voice, when she talks to her children about Jesus and his love, which stamps itself upon the heart, and the heart is a far better place for the custody of truth than ever the brain can become.

Too Little for the Lamb,
Volume 51, Sermon #2937 - Exodus 12:3, 4

Motivation

You are not acting as you ought to do when you are moved by any other motive than a single eye to your Lord's glory.

Morning and Evening, Page 644

To live for Jesus is to be swayed by the noblest of motives.

Words of Counsel, Page 87

The joy of doing good is found in the good itself; the reward of a deed of love is found in its own result.

Words of Counsel, Page 134

It is not what your hands are doing, nor even what your lips are saying; the main thing is what your heart is meaning and intending.

Love's Law and Life,
Volume 32, Sermon #1932 - John 14:15

Men do not do much if they act from mere feeling, and have no underlying design. Indeed, a life without an object must be a frivolous, useless life.

The Rule of the Race,
Volume 34, Sermon #2037 - Hebrews 12:1, 2

The true test of any action lies in its motive. Many a deed, which seems to be glorious, is really mean and ignoble because it is done with a base intention; while other actions, which appear to be poor and paltry, if we truly understood them, would be seen to be full of the glory and beauty of a noble purpose. The mainspring of a watch is the most important part of it; the spring of an action is everything.

Christ's Motive and Ours,
Volume 37, Sermon #2232 - 2 Corinthians 8:9, Philippians 1:29

It is not enough to do the correct thing, it must be done in a right spirit, and with a pure motive. A good action is not wholly good unless it be done for the glory of God, and because of the greatness and goodness of his holy name.

Forgiveness, Freedom, Favor,
Volume 38, Sermon #2276 - Deuteronomy 15:2

Gratitude ought to be, and I believe it is, in the heart the most powerful force in human motive.

Resurrection for the Just and the Unjust,
Volume 59, Sermon #3346 - Acts 24:15

Music

Heartless hymns are insults to heaven.

The Treasury of David, Psalm 45, Verse 1

Fine music without devotion is but a splendid garment upon a corpse.

The Treasury of David, Psalm 92, Verse 3

I am afraid that where organs, choirs, and singing men and singing women are left to do the praise of the congregation, men's minds are more occupied with the due performance of the music, than with the Lord, who alone is to be praised.

Praises and Vows Accepted in Zion,
Volume 17, Sermon #1023 - Psalm 65:1, 2

Brothers, we spoil our music by diverting our thoughts to man.

Jubilate,
Volume 31, Sermon #1867 - Exodus 15:1, 2

New Nature

None but God can create either a new heart or a new earth.

The Treasury of David, Psalm 51, Verse 10

Old things have passed away. He loves what he hated, and hates what he loved. He believes what he denied, and disbelieves what he formerly accepted.

Faith, and the Witness Upon Which It Is Founded,
Volume 21, Sermon #1213 - 1 John 5:8, 10

Have you been raised from death unto life? Have you been made to feel new emotions, new desires, new longings, new pains, and new joys?

Eternal Life!,
Volume 41, Sermon #2396 - John 17:3, 1 John 5:20, 21

God works in man a change so great that no reformation can even so much as thoroughly imitate it. It is an entire change—a change of the will, of the being, of the desires, of the hates, of the dislikings, and of the likings. In every respect the man becomes new when divine grace enters into his heart.

The Dumb Become Singers,
Volume 58, Sermon #3332 - Isaiah 35:6

Why, I think if some of us were to meet our old selves walking down the street, we should hardly know ourselves.

A Threefold Slogan,
Volume 62, Sermon #3536 - Luke 10:44, John 9:25, Philippians 3:13

Preparation for heaven consists still further in something that must be wrought in us, for observe, brethren, that if the Lord were to blot out all our sins we should still be quite incapable of entering heaven unless there was a change wrought in our natures.

Preparation for Heaven,
Volume 62, Sermon #3538 - 2 Corinthians 5:5

But, brethren, we cannot go to heaven as worldly men; for there would be nothing there to gratify us.

Preparation for Heaven,
Volume 62, Sermon #3538 - 2 Corinthians 5:5

Obedience

Things non-essential to salvation are nevertheless essential to obedience.

The Interest of Christ and His People in Each Other,
Volume 7, Sermon #374 - Song of Solomon 2:16

You and I must be willing to do what God tells us, as God tells us, when God tells us, because God tells us, but only strong faith will be equal to such complete obedience.

Strong Faith,
Volume 23, Sermon #1367 - Romans 4:20

Some Christians are very curious, but not obedient. Plain precepts are neglected, but difficult problems they seek to solve.

the Ascension and the Second Advent Practically Considered,
Volume 31, Sermon #1817 - Acts 1:10, 11

Do what the Lord bids you, where he bids you, as he bids you, as long as he bids you, and do it at once.

Peter's Blunder-A Lesson for Ourselves,
Volume 31, Sermon #1823 - Acts 10:14

Love is the chief jewel in the bracelet of obedience.

Love's Law and Life,
Volume 32, Sermon #1932 - John 14:15

Obedience rendered without delight in rendering it is only half obedience.

"Lo, I Come"-Application,
Volume 37, Sermon #2203 - Psalm 40:7

A great part of obedience lies in not doing.

Obeying Christ's Orders,
Volume 39, Sermon #2317 - John 2:5

A servant's true obedience can sometimes be as well seen in what he does not do, as in what he does.

God's Heart the Source of All Blessing,
Volume 45, Sermon #2641 - 2 Samuel 7:21

The less the thing is in itself, the more does it become the test of our obedience.

Examination Before Communion,
Volume 46, Sermon #2699 - 1 Corinthians 11:28

It seems to me that half the beauty of obedience consists in obeying the command at once.

Urging Lot,
Volume 51, Sermon #2944 - Genesis 19:15

To be obedient to God is the surest way to be victorious over wicked men! Keep God's Word and God will guard your head in the day of danger.

"The True Sayings of God",
Volume 55, Sermon #3144 - Revelation 19:9

No man is really saved unless he is in his heart obedient to Christ.

Prompt Obedience,
Volume 58, Sermon #3310 - Psalm 18:44

Objections

I confess that I do not believe that one human brain is capable of answering every objection that another human brain could raise against the most obvious truth in the world.

The Best Strengthening Medicine,
Volume 37, Sermon #2209 - Hebrews 11:34

To answer objections, is an endless task; it is like trying to empty a flowing fountain with bottomless buckets.

Blinded By Satan,
Volume 39, Sermon #2304 - 2 Corinthians 4:4

Old Age

From the altar of age the flashes of the fire of youth are gone, but the more real flame of earnest feeling remains.

Morning and Evening, Page 556

As we grow older, it is wise to concentrate more and more our energies upon the one thing, the only thing worth living for—the praise of God.

More and More,
Volume 17, Sermon #998 - Psalm 71:14

I always find that the older saints become more Calvinistic as they ripen in age; that is to say, they get to believe more and more that salvation is all of grace; and whereas, at first, they might have had some rather loose ideas concerning free-will, and the power of the creature, the lapse of years and fuller experience gradually blow all that kind of chaff away.

What We Have, and Are Have,
Volume 52, Sermon #2991 - 2 Thessalonians 2:16, 17

Old age should never be looked upon with dismay by us—it should be our joy.

Cheer for Despondency,
Volume 56, Sermon #3183 - Proverbs 27:1

Old Nature

The natural birth communicates nature's filthiness, but it cannot convey grace.

Come Ye Children, Page 22

The old nature never does improve, it is as earthly, and sensual, and devilish in the saint of eighty years of age as it was when he first came to Christ; it is unimproved and unimprovable; towards God it is enmity itself: every imagination of the thoughts of the heart is evil, and that continually.

The Withering Work of the Spirit,
Volume 17, Sermon #999 - Isaiah 40:6-8, 1 Peter 1:23-25

The eggs of all crimes are within our being: the accursed virus, from whose deadly venom every foul design will come, is present in the soul.

The Law Written in the Heart,
Volume 28, Sermon #1687 - Jeremiah 31:33

One of the best men I ever knew said, at eighty years of age, "I find the old man is not dead yet." Our old man is crucified, but he is long a-dying. He is not dead when we think he is. You may live to be very old; but you will have need still to watch against the carnal nature, which remains even in the regenerate.

Holy Longings,
Volume 36, Sermon #2151 - Psalm 119:131, 132, 133

There is not a complimentary word to human nature within the covers of the Bible.

Man Humbled, God Exalted,
Volume 59, Sermon #3369 - Isaiah 2:17

Men by nature need something to be done for them before they can enter heaven, and something to be done in them, something to be done with them, for by nature they are enemies of God.

Preparation for Heaven,
Volume 62, Sermon #3538 - 2 Corinthians 5:5

Opportunities

The wide awake man seizes opportunities or makes them, and thus those who are widest awake usually come to the front.

The Alarum,
Volume 17, Sermon #996 - Psalm 57:8

Paradoxes

What may seem defeat to us may be victory to Him.

Morning and Evening, Page 717

The difficulties about free agency and predestination have existed, do exist, and will exist to the world's end, ay, and through eternity too. Both facts are to my mind certain, but where they meet none knows but God himself.

Clearing the Road Heaven,
Volume 19, Sermon #1131 - Isaiah 62:10

What a strange medley are we of the diabolical and the divine, the sinful and the heavenly, so sadly wedded to the earth, and yet so gloriously born from heaven.

Thinking and Turning,
Volume 20, Sermon #1181 - Psalm 119:59

Do not let us exalt him into only a God-man; for if we do, we shall degrade him into a man-God. He is neither the one nor the other. He is God; diminish not his splendor. He is man,—man such as we are; forget not his tenderness.

"All of One",
Volume 41, Sermon #2418 - Hebrews 2:11-13

Oh, how many things you and I have still to gain by losing! How much we are to be enriched by our losses! How we are to make progress by going backward! How we have yet to mount by sinking! How we have yet to rise by descending!

The First and the Second,
Volume 46, Sermon #2698 - Hebrews 10:9

And you may depend upon this fact, that paradoxes are not strange things in Scripture, but are rather the rule than the exception.

Feeding On the Bread of Life,
Volume 46, Sermon #2706 - John 6:47, 48

You do not like to remember your sin; but, if you remember it, God will forget it; whereas, if you forget it, God will remember it against you.

The Great Miracle Worker,
Volume 47, Sermon #2736 - John 11:47

The sinner sins in order to be happy, as he thinks; and the newborn man abstains from sin in order to be happy.

Victorious Faith,
Volume 47, Sermon #2757 - 1 John 5:4, 5

Our war is for peace. Every blow that we strike is against blows. If we have to denounce anything, we do most of all denounce denunciation; and if we are bitter at all, most of all we are bitter against bitterness, and envy, and malice, and all uncharitableness.

Christ Before Annas,
Volume 49, Sermon #2820 - John 18:12, 13, 19-23

Permit me to use a paradox, and say that it is not trouble that troubles a man so much as something else that is the secret of the trouble.

The Cause and Effect of Heart Trouble,
Volume 54, Sermon #3076 - John 14:27

Parenting

Do not water your young plants either with vinegar or with syrup.

Only A Prayer Meeting, Page 108

A boy can be driven to learn till he loses half his wits: forced fruits have little flavor; a man at five is a fool at fifteen.

John Ploughman's Pictures, Page 71

Most men are what their mothers made them. The father is away from home all day, and has not half the influence over the children that the mother has.

John Ploughman's Pictures, Page 109

Little children give their mother the headache, but if she lets them have their own way, when they grow up to be great children they will give her the heartache.

John Ploughman's Pictures, Page 110

Soft-hearted mothers rear soft-headed children; they hurt them for life because they are afraid of hurting them when they are young.

John Ploughman's Pictures, Page 110

He who thinks it easy to bring up a family never had one of his own. A mother who trains her children aright had need be wiser than Solomon, for his son turned out a fool.

John Ploughman's Pictures, Page 111

A wild goose never lays a tame egg.

John Ploughman's Talk, Page 12

If you do not look to your actions, you may have good motives, but your example will not be very good. How necessary this is to the parent! because if the parent falls into an error, his children will imitate him in his vices far sooner than his virtues.

Heedlessness in Religion,
Volume 12, Sermon #685 - 2 Kings 10:31

You are a mother with little children, and it is probably your duty to be at home rather than to be at the prayer meeting. It may sometimes be your business, as a husband, to take turns with your wife, and let her come out to the house of God, instead of always taking the privilege yourself.

Peter's Three Calls,
Volume 12, Sermon #702 - John 1:37, Matthew 4:18, 19, 10:1, 2

We all agree with the remark that it is better to give a lad an education than a fortune, for the one he carries in him and cannot lose, but the other may soon be gone, since it is no part of himself.

Holy Water,
Volume 20, Sermon #1202 - John 4:14

Why, at home, to our children, especially when they are young, we are, as it were, little gods; they take their law from us, and their conduct is shaped according to the pattern we set before them.

A Holy and Homely Resolve,
Volume 21, Sermon #1230 - Psalm 101:2

May not your child's conduct to you be a fair reflection of your own conduct towards your heavenly Father?

For the Sick and Afflicted,
Volume 22, Sermon #1274 - Job 34:31, 32

What our boys need in starting in life is a God: if we have nothing else to give them, they have enough if they have God. What our girls want in quitting the nurture of home, is God's love in their hearts, and whether they have fortunes or not, is a small matter.

A Bit of History for Old and Young,
Volume 33, Sermon #1972 - Genesis 48:15, 16

Be ready to forgive your children.

Forgiveness, Freedom, Favor,
Volume 38, Sermon #2276 - Deuteronomy 15:2

You can generally read a man's character in his boy's face, and in his boy's conduct and conversation.

A Searching Question,
Volume 54, Sermon #3079 - 1 Samuel 30:13

Those children who are doted upon by their parents are greatly to be pitied, for they are apt to be allowed to have their own way, and a youth's own way is sure to be a wrong one.

The Old Testament "Prodigal",
Volume 59, Sermon #3354 - 2 Chronicles 33:12, 13

Brethren, if you wish to give your children a blessing when you die, be a blessing to them while you live. If you would make your last words worth the hearing, let your whole life be worth the seeing.

A Remarkable Benediction,
Volume 62, Sermon #3540 - Deuteronomy 33:16

Patience

We shall not grow weary of waiting upon God if we remember how long and how graciously He once waited for us.

Morning and Evening, Page 381

The disciples of a patient Savior should be patient themselves. Grin and bear it is the old-fashioned advice, but sing and bear it is a great deal better.

John Ploughman's Talk, Page 41

He who can wait long enough will win. This, that, and the other, anything, and everything, all put together make nothing in the end; but on one horse a man rides home in due season.

John Ploughman's Talk, Page 141

Patience! patience! you are always in a hurry, but God is not.

Joshua's Vision,
Volume 14, Sermon #795 - Joshua 5:13-15

To labour is not easy, but to labour and to wait is far harder.

The Northern Iron and the Steel,
Volume 17, Sermon #993 - Jeremiah 15:12

A fool soon makes up his mind, because there is so very little of it; but a wise man waits and considers.

On the Cross After Death,
Volume 33, Sermon #1956 - John 19:31-37

So, being himself a waiting God, he loves a waiting people; he loves a man who can take the promise, and say, "I believe it; it may never be fulfilled to me in this life, but I do not want that it should be. I am perfectly willing that it should be fulfilled when God intends that it should be."

The Two Pivots,
Volume 45, Sermon #2633 - Exodus 3:6, Hebrews 11:16

Peace

"In the world you shall have tribulation" is as sure fact as that in Christ you shall have peace!

Good Cheer from Christ's Victory over the World,
Volume 58, Sermon #3285 - John 16:33

Perfection

We are not perfect in character, any one of us—we are only perfect in position.

Perfection in Faith,
Volume 5, Sermon #232 - Hebrews 10:14

Now, Jesus comes in order that he may kill in you everything that is contrary to the mind of God; he comes to make you holy, to make you perfect.

A Prince and a Savior,
Volume 22, Sermon #1301 - Acts 5:31

"Must a man be perfect, then?" Sir, a man must desire to be perfect. "But he cannot be perfect." Sir, he can be perfect in intention, if not in fact, and there is a deal of difference between the sin of misadventure, and of infirmity, and the willfully wicked sin of some men.

Right-Hand Sins,
Volume 60, Sermon #3415 - Mark 9:43

He who boasts of being perfect is perfect in folly.

John Ploughman's Talk, Page 65

He is possessed of most devils who thinks he has the fewest imperfections, as a general rule.

Sihon and Og, Or Mercies in Detail,
Volume 22, Sermon #1285 - Psalm 136:27-22

I recollect when I resolved never to sin again. I sinned before I had done my breakfast.

The Sinner Saved,
Volume 33, Sermon #1961 - Romans 9:30-33

No one is so imperfect in temper as the perfect man; he soon shows his imperfection.

God's People Melted and Tried,
Volume 38, Sermon #2274 - Jeremiah 9:7

When I meet with a brother who tells me that he is nearly perfect, I know that he is living in the dark; for, if he lived in the light, he would see how far short he came of the glory of God.

"Going and Weeping",
Volume 53, Sermon #3049 - Jeremiah 50:4

Whenever you hear a man boast that he is holy, remember that good scent needs no proclaiming.

Concentration and Diffusion,
Volume 55, Sermon #3174 - John 12:3

To be fit for heaven a man must be perfect. Go, you who think you can prepare yourselves, be perfect for a day.

Preparation for Heaven,
Volume 62, Sermon #3538 - 2 Corinthians 5:5

Perseverance of the Saints

This faithfulness of God is the foundation and cornerstone of our hope of final perseverance. The saints shall persevere in holiness because God perseveres in grace. He perseveres to bless, and there believers persevere in being blessed. He continues to keep His people, and there they continue to keep His commandments.

All of Grace, Page 122

Perseverance is the badge of true saints. The Christian life is not a beginning only in the ways of God, but also a continuance in the same as long as life lasts. It is with a Christian as it was with the great Napoleon: he said, "Conquest has made me what I am, and conquest must maintain me."

Morning and Evening, Page 295

Christian, it is not with you that you may persevere or not—it is not an optional blessing—you must persevere, or else all you have ever known and felt will be good for nothing to you. You must hold on your way if you are ultimately to be saved.

The Righteous Holding on His Way,
Volume 13, Sermon #749 - Job 17:9

Conversion is a turning into the right road; the next thing is to walk in it. The daily going on in that road is as essential as the first starting if you would reach the desired end. To strike the first blow is not all the battle; to him that overcomes the crown is promised. To start in the race is nothing, many have done that who have failed; but to hold out till you reach the winning post is the great point of the matter. Perseverance is as necessary to a man's salvation as conversion.

Life's Need and Maintenance,
Volume 22, Sermon #1300 - Psalm 22:29

The saints prove their conversion by their perseverance, and that perseverance comes from a continual supply of divine grace to their souls.

The Candle,
Volume 27, Sermon #1594 - Matthew 5:15, 16

Final perseverance is the necessary evidence of genuine conversion.

The Watchword for Today—"Stand Fast",
Volume 33, Sermon #1959 - Philippians 3:20, 21;4:1

We believe in the perseverance of the saints, but many are not saints, and therefore do not persevere. Nominal saints exhibit no final perseverance.

Truth Stranger Than Fiction,
Volume 35, Sermon #2081 - Joel 2:25

Temporary Christians are no Christians: only the believer who continues to believe will enter heaven.

The Covenant Promise of the Spirit,
Volume 37, Sermon #2200 - Ezekiel 36:27

Persistence

To plod on under apparent failure is one of the most acceptable of all works of faith, and he who can do it year after year is assuredly well-pleasing unto God.

Words of Counsel, Page 86

Die in harness if your mental and physical vigor will permit.

Words of Counsel, Page 95

The difficulty of the Christian is very seldom the commencement of the work; the true labour lies in the perseverance which alone can win the victory.

The Former and the Latter Rain,
Volume 15, Sermon #880 - Jeremiah 5:24

In the long run stay is the winning virtue; he that endures to the end the same shall be saved.

Motives for Steadfastness,
Volume 19, Sermon #1111 - 1 Corinthians 15:58

Activity often makes up for a lack of ability.

Cheer Up, My Comrades!,
Volume 26, Sermon #1513 - 2 Chronicles 35:2

He is surest to succeed who cannot be put off from his aim.

Our Great Shepherd Finding the Sheep,
Volume 35, Sermon #2065 - Luke 15:4, 5, 6

I never can comprehend how the snails managed to get into the ark, yet they did; they must have started very early.

Preparing for the Week of Prayer,
Volume 57, Sermon #3282 - Revelation 8:3, 4

Pleasure

Rest assured, dear friends, that where your pleasure is, there your heart is.

Christ the Cause of Division,
Volume 47, Sermon #2710 - John 7:43

Praise

It is your duty to praise him.

A Lecture for Little-Faith,
Volume 4, Sermon #205 - 2 Thessalonians 1:3

If you cannot magnify God, it is probably because you are magnifying yourself.

The Keynote of a Choice Sonnet,
Volume 26, Sermon #1514 - Luke 1:46

As soon as a man is cleansed from sin, he is clothed with praise.

A Great Gospel for Great Sinners,
Volume 31, Sermon #1837 - 1 Timothy 1:15-17

Prayer is not so heavenly an exercise as praise; prayer is for time, the ever-blessed One; yet it is so, for he has declared that he is well pleased with the praises and the gifts of his children.

A Life-Long Occupation,
Volume 34, Sermon #2048 - Hebrews 13:15

You cannot always be speaking his praise, but you can always be living his praise.

A Life-Long Occupation,
Volume 34, Sermon #2048 - Hebrews 13:15

The ungodly are not half so restrained in their blasphemy as we are in our praise.

Joy, Joy forever,
Volume 36, Sermon #2146 - Psalm 5:11

We can bless God by praising him, extolling him, desiring all honor for him, ascribing all good to him, magnifying and lauding his holy name.

Blessing for Blessing,
Volume 38, Sermon #2266 - Ephesians 1:3, 4

A rejoicing heart soon makes a praising tongue.

Howling Changed to Singing,
Volume 39, Sermon #2310 - Psalm 13:1, 2, 6

If you do not feel you can bless him for the present moment, yet forget not to bless him for the past; and when you once begin to do that, you will soon find that your praise will overlap the past, and cover the present, if it does not even run into the future.

Three Blessings of the Heavenly Charter,
Volume 39, Sermon #2314 - Job 10:12

Praise is the beauty of a Christian. What wings are to a bird, what fruit is to the tree, what the rose is to the thorn, that is praise to a child of God.

Prayer, the Proof of Godliness,
Volume 41, Sermon #2437 - Psalm 32:6

Praise is the end of prayer and preaching.

Alto and Bass,
Volume 44, Sermon #2582 - Luke 1:53

Remember that, if you do not praise God, it is impossible for you ever to enter heaven, for that is the chief occupation of heaven; and remember also that praise from your lips, until those lips are divinely cleansed, would be like a jewel in a swine's snout, a thing altogether out of place.

Jude's Doxology,
Volume 52, Sermon #2994 - Jude 1:24, 25

To praise God without praying to Him would be impossible. To pray to God without praising Him would be ungrateful.

God in Heaven, and Men on the Sea,
Volume 58, Sermon #3321 - Psalm 65:5

Prayer

Prayer is one of the necessary wheels of the machinery of providence.

An All Around Ministry, Page 12

We cannot all argue, but we can all pray; we cannot all be leaders, but we can all be pleaders; we cannot all be mighty in rhetoric, but we can all be prevalent in prayer.

An All Around Ministry, Page 314

Prayer irrigates the fields of life with the waters which are stored up in the reservoirs of promise.

According to Promise, Page 59

Prayer is the thermometer of grace.

Barbed Arrows, Page 210

Our God not only hears prayer but also loves to hear it.

Morning and Evening, Page 616

Believe me, if a church does not pray, it is dead.

The Greatest Fight in the World, Page 43

Election is the guarantee of complete salvation, and an argument for success at the throne of grace. He who chose us for himself will surely hear our prayers.

The Treasury of David, Psalm 4, Verse 3

Prayer may be answered in anger and denied in love.

The Treasury of David, Psalm 106, Verse 15

We pray best when we are fallen on our faces in painful helplessness.

The Treasury of David, Psalm 107, Verse 13

Words are but the habitation of prayer, the living tenant is desire.

Words of Advice, Page 154

Live and die without prayer, and you will pray long enough when you get to hell.

Words of Cheer, Page 8

Prayer will make you leave off sinning, or sinning will make you leave off praying.

Paul's First Prayer,
Volume 1, Sermon #16 - Acts 9:11

He can reverse nature, but he cannot reverse his own nature, and he must do this before he can forebear to hear and answer prayer.

A Sermon for the Week of Prayer,
Volume 7, Sermon #354 - Colossians 4:2

Many hours are spent with men, how many with your Maker?

Hindrances to Prayer,
Volume 20, Sermon #1192 - 1 Peter 3:7

The law of gravitation I might doubt, but the law that God hears prayer I cannot doubt.

Opening the Mouth,
Volume 21, Sermon #1221 - Psalm 81:10

God will not give you what you cannot receive or put to healthy use.

Opening the Mouth,
Volume 21, Sermon #1221 - Psalm 81:10

Our cup is small, and we blame the fountain.

Opening the Mouth,
Volume 21, Sermon #1221 - Psalm 81:10

The way to have enquiring sinners is for us to become enquiring saints.

Enquire of the Lord,
Volume 22, Sermon #1304 - Ezekiel 36:37, 38

Teach us, thy children, to be always talking with thee, so that while we walk on earth our conversation may be in heaven.

The Secret of A Happy Life,
Volume 22, Sermon #1305 - Psalm 16:8

The essence of prayer lies in the heart drawing near to God: and it can do that without words.

The Reason Why Many Cannot Find,
Volume 24, Sermon #1408 - James 4:7-10

Coming events cast their shadows before them, and when God is about to bless his people, his coming favor casts the shadow of prayer over the church.

The Holy Spirit's Intercession,
Volume 26, Sermon #1532 - Romans 8:26, 27

Prayer is not meant for the Lord's information. The question is not put to you that you may instruct him, but that he may instruct you.

Jesus Knew What He Would Do,
Volume 27, Sermon #1605 - John 6:6

That patience which does not pray is obstinacy. A soul silent to God is apt to be sullen rather than submissive.

Brought Up from the Horrible Pit,
Volume 28, Sermon #1674 - Psalm 40:1-3

Holiness is essential to power in prayer: the life must knock while the lips ask and the heart seeks.

"Knock!",
Volume 29, Sermon #1723 - Matthew 7:12

The act of prayer is blessed, the habit of prayer is more blessed, but the spirit of prayer is the most blessed of all; and it is this that we can continue for months and years.

Spiritual Knowledge and Its Practical Results,
Volume 29, Sermon #1742 - Colossians 1:9, 10

The less prayer is observed on earth, the more it is observed in heaven.

Before Daybreak with Christ,
Volume 30, Sermon #1769 - Mark 1:35-39

Prayer is the autograph of the Holy Ghost upon the renewed heart.

"Behold, He Prays",
Volume 31, Sermon #1860 - Acts 9:11

It is a good fall when a man falls on his knees.

Song for the Free-Hope for the Bound,
Volume 33, Sermon #1992 - Psalm 107:14-16

Prayer is the natural out gushing of a soul in communion with Jesus.

The Secret of Power in Prayer,
Volume 34, Sermon #2002 - John 15:7

True prayer is measured by weight, not by length. A single groan before God may have more fullness of prayer in it than a fine oration of great length.

The Secret of Power in Prayer,
Volume 34, Sermon #2002 - John 15:7

When your heart is like a boiling geyser, let it steam aloft in pillars of prayer.

Concerning Prayer,
Volume 34, Sermon #2053 - Psalm 86:6, 7

Prayer is the thermometer of Divine Grace.

A Call to Prayer and Testimony,
Volume 37, Sermon #2189 - Isaiah 62:6, 7

Prayer is dealing with God.

A Poor Man's Cry—And What Came of It,
Volume 37, Sermon #2193 - Psalm 34:6

Though infinitely better able to do without prayer than we are, yet Jesus prayed much more than we do.

Our Lord in the Valley of Humiliation,
Volume 38, Sermon #2281 - Philippians 2:8

There are two prayers always worth praying, "Lord, show me myself," and "Lord, show me thyself." May both be heard, and you will be well taught of God!

God's Pupil, God's Preacher—An Autobiography,
Volume 39, Sermon #2318 - Psalm 71:17

Prayer is not for God's information, but for our instruction!

A Page from a Royal Diary,
Volume 40, Sermon #2372 - Psalm 119:132

If you are going to die, die praying! Do not let The Fear of Death stop your praying, that would be folly, indeed!

Heman's Sorrowful Psalm,
Volume 41, Sermon #2433 - Psalm 88:13

Brothers and Sisters, pray for us, and pray for all the preachers of the Word, that they may be stars in the right hand of Christ!

A Portrait No Artist Can Paint,
Volume 43, Sermon #2498 - Revelation 1:16

No matter what sorrow falls to your lot, if you can pray, you will rise out of it.

Refusing to Be Comforted,
Volume 44, Sermon #2578 - Psalm 77:2

How often have I said that prayer is the breathing in of the air of heaven, and praise is the breathing of it out again.

A Visit from the Lord,
Volume 44, Sermon #2599 - Psalm 106:4

A true prayer is the echo of the eternal purpose of God.

"Pray, Always Pray",
Volume 48, Sermon #2800 - John 16:26, 27

It matters little what other power you possess; if you have no power with God, you are powerless.

"Pray, Always Pray",
Volume 48, Sermon #2800 - John 16:26, 27

A prayer without Christ in it will never reach Heaven!

The Lesson of Uzza,
Volume 49, Sermon #2855 - 1 Chronicles 13:8, 12;15:25

Prayer is a living thing—you cannot find a living prayer in a dead heart. Why seek you the living among the dead, or search the sepulcher to find the signs and tokens of life? No, Sir, if you have not been made alive by the Grace of God, you cannot pray!

Prayer Found in the Heart,
Volume 50, Sermon #2869 - 2 Samuel 7:27

Brothers and Sisters, if we had more sense of our need, prayer would be more of an instinct with us—we would pray because we could not help praying!

The Wide-Open Mouth Filled,
Volume 50, Sermon #2879 - Psalm 81:10

Some men go to God and ask only for temporal favors and, possibly, they do not obtain them. He who would be content with this world will probably never get it—but he who craves spiritual good may ask with the absolute certainty of receiving it!

The Wide-Open Mouth Filled,
Volume 50, Sermon #2879 - Psalm 81:10

Prayerless souls are Christless souls, Christless souls are Graceless souls and Graceless souls shall soon be damned souls. See your peril, you that neglect altogether the blessed privilege of prayer! You are in the bonds of iniquity, you are in the gall of bitterness. God deliver you, for His name's sake!

Restraining Prayer,
Volume 51, Sermon #2943 - Job 15:4

It is a great help in prayer, when you are yourself unable to pray, to get someone whom you know to be a Christian, and who has sympathy with you, to come and pray with you.

Christ's Death and Ours,
Volume 53, Sermon #3024 - John 12:23-24

Prayer is the indispensable mark of the true child of God.

Pedigree,
Volume 54, Sermon #3091 - 2 Corinthians 11:22

You are no Christian if you do not pray. A prayerless soul is a Christless soul.

Pedigree,
Volume 54, Sermon #3091 - 2 Corinthians 11:22

Often, when a Believer groans in prayer and cannot pray, he has offered the best prayer.

Good Cheer From Christ's Real Presence,
Volume 55, Sermon #3128 - Mark 6:45-52

Dear young people, take care that you start right in your Christian life by being much in prayer! A profession of faith that does not begin with prayer will end in disgrace. If you come to join the Church, but do not pray to God to uphold you in consistency of life, and to make your profession sincere, the probability is that you are already a hypocrite!

The Preparatory of Prayers of Christ,
Volume 56, Sermon #3178 - Luke 3:21, 22; 6:12, 13; 9:28, 29,
Matthew 14:23-25, John 11:41, 42, Luke 22:31, 32; 23:46

It is not recorded that His disciples ever said to Him, "Lord, teach us how to preach," but at least one of them was so struck with His prayers that he said, "Lord, teach us to pray."

A Sermon for A Winter's Evening,
Volume 56, Sermon #3181 - John 18:18

No one begins to live the life of faith who has not also begun to pray—and as prayer is necessary at the commencement of the Christian career, so is it necessary all through. A Christian's vigor, happiness, growth and usefulness all depend upon prayer.

Boldness at the Throne,
Volume 56, Sermon #3182 - Hebrews 4:16

One drop of Christ's blood upon a prayer must make it prosper.

Peter's Shortest Prayer,
Volume 56, Sermon #3186 - Matthew 14:30

It is not a matter of time so much as a matter of heart; if you have the heart to pray, you will find the time.

Peter's Shortest Prayer,
Volume 56, Sermon #3186 - Matthew 14:30

The habit of daily prayer must be maintained. It is well to have regular hours of devotion and to resort to the same place for prayer, as far as possible. Still, the spirit of prayer is better than the habit of prayer. It is better to be able to pray at all times than to make it a rule to pray at certain times and seasons.

Peter's Shortest Prayer,
Volume 56, Sermon #3186 - Matthew 14:30

That is the short road to true knowledge—to pray. Study is good, no doubt, for the acquisition of knowledge. But praying is the best way to obtain true wisdom!

A Command and a Promise,
Volume 56, Sermon #3212 - James 4:8

When we cease to pray for blessings, God has already ceased to bless us— but when our souls pour out floods of prayer, God is certain to pour out floods of mercy.

The Blood of Christ's Covenant,
Volume 57, Sermon #3240 - Zechariah 9:11

When you feel disinclined to pray, let it be a sign to you that prayer is doubly necessary! Pray for prayer!

The Sealed Hand—A Winter Sermon,
Volume 58, Sermon #3289 - Job 37:7

It may be said, "We can pray at all times." I know we can; but I fear that those who do not pray at stated hours seldom pray at all.

The Broken Fence,
Volume 59, Sermon #3381 - Proverbs 24:30-32

May we not draw some comfort from the thought that our prayers never are intrusions?

A Definite Challenge for Definite Prayer,
Volume 62, Sermon #3537 - Mark 10:51

Preaching

We hear complaints that the minister speaks too harshly and talks too much of judgment. Saved sinners never make that complaint.

The Ship on Fire—A Voice of Warning,
Volume 10, Sermon #550 - Genesis 19:17, 19

It is a remarkable fact, that where the gospel is not preached in its general aspect, God does not seem to work out his special object to any large extent.

General and Yet Particular,
Volume 10, Sermon #566 - John 17:2

Surely if men's hearts were right, short sermons would be enough.

The Parable of the Wedding Feast,
Volume 17, Sermon #975 - Matthew 22:2, 3, 4

A sermon without Christ as its beginning, middle, and end is a mistake in conception and a crime in execution.

Without Christ—Nothing,
Volume 27, Sermon #1625 - John 15:5

If you always enjoy sermons, the minister is not a good steward. He is not acting wisely who deals out nothing but sweets.

The Mediator—The Interpreter,
Volume 35, Sermon #2097 - Exodus 20:18-20

If the Lord's bearing our sin for us is not the gospel, I have no gospel to preach.

The Burden of the Word of the Lord,
Volume 35, Sermon #2114 - Malachi 1:1

The best help you can give men socially is to help them religiously—and the best religious help is to preach the Gospel to them.

Belief, Baptism, Blessing,
Volume 38, Sermon #2275 - Acts 16:33, 34

The backbone of the preaching of Christ is a conviction of the Truth of Christ.

Paul, the Ready,
Volume 38, Sermon #2285 - Romans 1:15

The most effective sermons are those which make opposers of the Gospel bite their lips and gnash their teeth.

"The Offense of the Cross",
Volume 44, Sermon #2594 - Galatians 5:11

Whenever we want to have converts—and I hope that is always—the best thing for us to do is to "preach the Word." There is nothing better! There can be nothing more—there must be nothing less!

Revelation and Conversion,
Volume 50, Sermon #2870 - Psalm 19:7

When the Spirit of God goes with the Word, then the Word becomes the instrument of the conversion of the souls of men.

Revelation and Conversion,
Volume 50, Sermon #2870 - Psalm 19:7

The true teacher should not seek to soar on the gaudy wings of brilliant oratory, pouring forth sonorous polished sentences in rhythmic harmony, but should endeavor to speak pointed Truths of God—things that will strike and stick—thoughts that will be remembered and recalled, again and again, when the hearer is far away from the place of worship where he listened to the preacher's words.

The Wide-Open Mouth Filled,
Volume 50, Sermon #2879 - Psalm 81:10

Christ's ministers may all go home, for their office is useless, if there is no forgiveness of sins!

Forgiveness and Fear,
Volume 50, Sermon #2882 - Psalm 130:4

I like to think about how many people are going to be saved every time the Gospel is faithfully preached. It is not preached in vain—we deliver a message from God that never misses the mark at which He aimed it!

"To You",
Volume 50, Sermon #2899 - Acts 13:26

There were great preachers before Luther and Calvin, before Wickliffe and Huss and Jerome—they went about preaching and preaching to great crowds, too, but they did not save souls! That was not because they could not speak and were not attractive, but because they had not this story to tell—the story that is in this Book—the story of Him who did hang upon the Cross.

An Old-Fashioned Remedy,
Volume 51, Sermon #2921 - Psalm 107:20

I had sooner die than live to be such a being as many who stand up in the pulpit wholly to waste people's time and not to win souls!

Warning and Encouragement,
Volume 52, Sermon #3013 - Song of Solomon 5:2

The more of Scripture, yes, of the very words of Scripture that we can use in preaching, the better and, certainly, the more of such thing as can begin with, "Thus says the Lord."

Heart Piercing,
Volume 54, Sermon #3094 - Acts 2:37

If you cannot preach at home because your practice runs counter to your preaching, do not preach at all—for a man has no right to talk and instruct others it he cannot, at least in some measure, live out what he teaches!

A Pastoral Visit,
Volume 54, Sermon #3103 - Philemon 1:2

When we preach Christ crucified, we have no reason to stammer, or stutter, or hesitate, or apologize; there is nothing in the gospel of which we have any cause to be ashamed.

Preaching Christ Crucified,
Volume 56, Sermon #3218 - 1 Corinthians 1:23

The same sun which melts wax hardens clay.

God's Firebrands,
Volume 57, Sermon #3233 - Zechariah 3:2

Shame on the preacher who does not bend the bow with all his might and throw his whole strength of spirit, soul and body into his efforts to win souls!

Satan's Arrows and God's,
Volume 57, Sermon #3262 - Lamentations 3:12, 13

Pride

We can be very high and mighty, if we please; and the smaller we are, the more easily do we swell out.

An All Around Ministry, Page 269

The Lord loves to use tools which are not rusted with self-conceit.

Barbed Arrows, Page 280

There's always time to boast—wait a little longer.

John Ploughman's Talk, Page 57

A man's praise smells sweet when it comes out of other men's mouths, but in his own it stinks.

John Ploughman's Talk, Page 155

The moment we glorify ourselves, since there is room for one glory only in the universe, we set ourselves up as rivals to the Most High.

Morning and Evening, Page 458

That demon of pride was born with us, and it will not die one hour before us.

Fear Not,
Volume 3, Sermon #156 - Isaiah 41:14

Ye shall not have his smiles if the smiles of the world will do as well.

The Blessed Guest Detained,
Volume 28, Sermon #1655 - Luke 24:28, 29

So much remains to be accomplished that we have no time to consider what has been done.

To Lovers of Jesus—An Example,
Volume 31, Sermon #1834 - Mark 14:6

One's pride may carry him far if he is a great fool; but let him not suffer his pride to carry him into hell, for it certainly will never carry him out again.

To Those Who Are Angry with Their Godly Friends,
Volume 32, Sermon #1929 - Genesis 4:6, 7

We know many persons who are always doing a great deal, and yet do nothing; fussy people, people to the front in every movement, persons who could set the whole world right, but are not right themselves.

The Unkept Vineyard-Or, Personal Work Neglected,
Volume 32, Sermon #1936 - Song of Solomon 1:6

God has made something of you, and now you are too respectable to look after those who are no worse than you were once.

Christ's Connection with Sinners the Source of His Glory,
Volume 35, Sermon #2070 - Isaiah 53:12

When a man admires himself he never adores God.

The Eye and the Light,
Volume 35, Sermon #2109 - Luke 11:33-36

The difficulty with some people is that they are always wanting to practice the sublime.

A Gracious Dismissal,
Volume 37, Sermon #2183 - Luke 7:50

How gentle and tender ought we to be with others who are foolish when we remember how foolish we are ourselves!

God's Knowledge of Sin,
Volume 44, Sermon #2551 - Psalm 69:5

So do not destroy your own strength by taking the glory of it to yourself.

The Glory of Our Strength,
Volume 55, Sermon #3140 - Psalm 89:17

Whatever God gives thee be grateful for, for if too proud to take from the raven's mouth, it will be well for thee to go without, until thine hunger consume thy pride.

God's Care of Elijah,
Volume 57, Sermon #3264 - 1 Kings 17:4

A man never lowers himself more than when he tries to lift himself up.

Good Talk,
Volume 60, Sermon #3399 - 1 Chronicles 16:9

Procrastination

He that has time, and looks for better time, time comes that he repents himself of time.

John Ploughman's Talk, Page 52

Remember that, if you have missed Christ by but the ticking of a clock, you have missed Christ for ever; so that minutes and ticks of clocks may be invested with a very solemn power, if we come to look at them in that light.

Delay Is Dangerous,
Volume 13, Sermon #772 - Genesis 24:55

Delay is the devil's great net. All men mean to repent. Alas! they will repent one day that they did not repent at once.

Crowding to Touch the Savior,
Volume 14, Sermon #841 - Mark 3:10

Life is like an evening; the longer you wait the darker it becomes. Delay bristles with danger, and the best fruit it can possibly bear is regret.

One Lion, Two Lions, No Lion At All!,
Volume 28, Sermon #1670 - Proverbs 22:13; 26:13

Probably the worst people in the world are those who have the best intentions, but never carry them out.

The Sluggard's Farm,
Volume 34, Sermon #2027 - Proverbs 24:30-32

To-morrow! oh, that cursed word to-morrow! How has man made it cursed! I find it not in the almanack of the wise; it is only in the calendar of fools. To-morrow! there is no such thing except in dreamland, for when that comes which we call to-morrow it will be to-day, and still for ever to- day, to-day, to-day. There is no time but that which is. Time was, is not, and time to come, is not.

The Call of "Today",
Volume 55, Sermon #3160 - Hebrews 3:7

Providence

To suppose that temporal things are too little for our condescending God, is to forget that he observes the flight of sparrows, and counts the hairs of his people's heads. Besides, everything is so little to him, that, if he does not care for the little, he cares for nothing.

According to Promise, Page 102

There is as much providence in the creeping of an aphis upon a rose leaf as in the marching of an army to ravage a continent.

A Good Start, Page 94

Blessed is the man who sees God in trifles! It is there that it is the hardest to see him; but he who believes that God is there, may go from the little providence up to the God of providence.

Providence,
Volume 4, Sermon #187 - Matthew 10:30

To gather up all in one, the calamities of earthquake, the devastations of storm, the extirpations of war, and all the terrible catastrophes of plague, have only been co-workers with God— slave compelled to tug the galley of the divine purpose across the sea of time.

The Infallibility of God's Purpose,
Volume 7, Sermon #406 - Job 23:13

No life can surpass that of a man who quietly continues to serve God in the place where providence has placed him.

Enoch,
Volume 22, Sermon #1307 - Genesis 5:21-24, Hebrews 11:5, 6, Jude 1:14, 15

Regeneration

To fashion a world has less difficulty in it than to create a new life in an ungodly man; for, in the creation of the world, there was nothing in the way of God; but, in the creation of the new heart, there is the old nature opposing the Spirit.

An All Around Ministry, Page 325

The grace which does not make a man better than others is a worthless counterfeit.

Morning and Evening, Page 79

Those who are saved by God the Holy Spirit are created anew according to Scripture; but who ever dreamed of creation creating itself? God spoke the world out of nothing, but nothing did not aid in the creation of the universe. Divine energy can do everything, but what can nothing do? Now if we have a new creation, there must have been a creator, and it is clear that being then spiritually created, we could not have assisted in our own new creation, unless, indeed, death can assist life, and non-existence aid in creation.

Salvation Altogether By Grace,
Volume 12, Sermon #703 - 2 Timothy 1:9

No strength but that which made me can new-make me.

The Sitting of the Refiner,
Volume 27, Sermon #1575 - Malachi 3:3

After we are regenerated, he continues to renew us; our thoughts, feelings, desires, and acts are constantly renewed. Regeneration as the commencement of the new creation can never come twice to any man, but renewal of the Holy Ghost is constantly and perpetually repeated.

The Maintenance of Good Works,
Volume 34, Sermon #2042 - Titus 3:3-8

Relationships

Depend upon it, a great deal depends upon whom we choose for our companions when we begin life.

Come Ye Children, Page 121

Beware of trusting all your secrets with anybody but your wife.

John Ploughman's Pictures, Page 118

Commit all your secrets to no man; trust in God with all your heart, but let your confidence in friends be weighed in the balances of prudence, seeing that men are but men, and all men are frail. Trust not great weights to slender threads.

John Ploughman's Talk, Page 58

It is foolish to turn off a tried friend because of a failing or two, for you may get rid of a one-eyed nag and buy a blind one.

John Ploughman's Talk, Page 67

Be friendly to all, but make none your friends until they know you, and you know them.

A Faithful Friend,
Volume 3, Sermon #120 - Proverbs 18:24

I fear that some men would sooner be damned than be laughed at.

Pilate and Ourselves Guilty of the Savior's Death,
Volume 28, Sermon #1648 - Matthew 27:24, 25

Grace builds neither monasteries nor nunneries.

"A Little Sanctuary",
Volume 34, Sermon #2001 - Ezekiel 11:16

We would have as our associates people who are established by principle rather than moved by passion.

By the Fountain,
Volume 35, Sermon #2113 - Genesis 39:22, Deuteronomy 32:13

Repentance

Repentance will not make you see Christ, but to see Christ will give you repentance.

All of Grace, Page 72

Repentance makes us see the evil of sin, not merely as a theory, but experimentally—as a burnt child dreads fire.

Morning and Evening, Page 574

Sincere repentance is continual. Believers repent until their dying day. This dropping well is not intermittent.

Morning and Evening, Page 574

"Only a change of mind"; but what a change! A change of mind with regard to everything! Instead of saying, "It is only a change of mind," it seems to me more truthful to say it is a great and deep change—even a change of the mind itself.

The Soul Winner, Page 31

True regeneration implants a hatred of all evil; and where one sin is delighted in, the evidence is fatal to a sound hope.

The Soul Winner, Page 33

It is not so much said, "turn our captivity," but turn "us." All will come right if we are right.

The Treasury of David, Psalm 80, Verse 3

A Christian must never leave off repenting, for I fear he never leaves off sinning.

Gray Hairs,
Volume 14, Sermon #830 - Hosea 7:9

He who looks sin ward has his back to God—he who looks Godward has his back to sin.

Conversions Desired,
Volume 22, Sermon #1282 - Acts 11:21

The true penitent repents of sin against God, and he would do so even if there were no punishment. When he is forgiven, he repents of sin more than ever; for he sees more clearly than ever the wickedness of offending so gracious a God.

Beginning at Jerusalem,
Volume 29, Sermon #1729 - Luke 24:47

God gives repentance, but men must themselves repent.

God's Work Upon Minister and Convert,
Volume 30, Sermon #1774 - Acts 26:16-20

The man who only repents of this and that glaring offense, has not repented of sin at all.

Two Essential Things,
Volume 35, Sermon #2073 - Acts 20:21

Beloved, true repentance is sorrow for the sin itself: it has not only a dread of the death which is the wages of sin, but of the sin which earns the wages.

Two Essential Things,
Volume 35, Sermon #2073 - Acts 20:21

Remember, Sinner, that there will never be a tear of acceptable repentance in your eyes till you have first looked to Jesus Christ!

"Jesus Wept",
Volume 35, Sermon #2091 - John 11:35

There is, in the world, a great deal of sorrow on account of sin which is certainly not repentance, and never leads to it.

Sorrow and Sorrow,
Volume 46, Sermon #2691 - 2 Corinthians 7:10

We do not repent in order to be saved, but we repent because we are saved. We do not loathe sin and, therefore, hope to be saved, but, because we are saved, we therefore loathe sin and turn altogether from it.

Mistaken Notions About Repentance,
Volume 47, Sermon #2743 - Ezekiel 36:21

It is always a sign of repentance in Christians who have fallen when they leave the company where they were led astray.

Peter's Fall and Restoration,
Volume 48, Sermon #2771 - Luke 22:61, 62

There was never any real godly sorrow which worked repentance acceptable to God except that which was the result of the Holy Spirit's own work within the soul.

Mourning At the Cross,
Volume 50, Sermon #2901 - Zechariah 12:10

That faith which is not accompanied by repentance will have to be repented of!

The Plumb Line,
Volume 50, Sermon #2904 - Amos 7:7, 8

You would not teach your children, I suppose, to say their prayers backwards and begin at, "Amen." and you are beginning at the wrong end when you want, first of all, to know your election instead of commencing with repentance towards God and faith in our Lord Jesus Christ!

Election—Its Defenses and Evidences,
Volume 51, Sermon #2920 - 1 Thessalonians 1:4-6

Remember this—there never was a saint who repented as much as he should have, for repentance should be perfect and no Christian has ever attained to that height.

Enquiring the Way to Zion,
Volume 53, Sermon #3035 - Jeremiah 50:5

Repentance is necessary in every case; there must be this radical change which shall make you loathe what you once loved, and love what you once loathed.

The Necessity of Regeneration,
Volume 54, Sermon #3121 - John 3:7

Repentance and faith are distasteful to the unregenerate; they would sooner repeat a thousand formal prayers than shed a solitary tear of true repentance.

The Necessity of Regeneration,
Volume 54, Sermon #3121 - John 3:7

The servants of Christ are not to preach repentance on their own authority, or even on the authority of the Church of Christ, but they are to preach it on the authority of the Church's ascended Head!

"Repentance and Remission",
Volume 56, Sermon #3224 - Luke 24:47

Every child of God is born-again with a tear in his or her eyes. Dry-eyed faith is not the faith of God's elect. He who rejoices in Christ, at the same time mourns for sin! Repentance is joined to faith by loving bonds, as the Siamese twins were united in one.

Solace for Sad Hearts,
Volume 58, Sermon #3325 - Isaiah 61:3

Wherever there is a real forgiveness of sin, there will be real sorrow on account of it.

Penitence, Pardon and Peace,
Volume 59, Sermon #3359 - Luke 7:37-38

Revenge

If you can revenge yourself, DON'T. If you could do it as easily as open your hand, keep it shut! If one bitter word could end the argument, ask for Divine Grace to spare that bitter word.

The Mission of Affliction,
Volume 55, Sermon #3164 - 2 Samuel 16:11, 12

Salvation

Watch with ceaseless care over those new-born babes who are strong in desires, but strong in nothing else.

Come Ye Children, Page 6

Whether we teach young Christians truth or not, the devil will be sure to teach them error.

Come Ye Children, Page 9

We know that infants enter the kingdom, for we are convinced that all of our race who die in infancy are included in the election of grace, and partake in the redemption wrought out by our Lord Jesus.

Come Ye Children, Page 37

If the Savior has not sanctified you, renewed you, given you a hatred of sin and a love of holiness, He has nothing in you of a saving character.

Morning and Evening, Page 79

God never clothes men until He has first stripped them, nor does He quicken them by the gospel till first they are slain by the law.

The Soul Winner, Page 28

Nothing will last to eternity, but that which came from eternity.

Words of Warning, Page 76

In the first birth—born to sin, in the next—born to holiness; in the first—partakers of corruption, in the next—heirs of incorruption; in the first— depravity, in the second—perfection.

The New Nature,
Volume 7, Sermon #398 - 1 Peter 1:23-25

I think it very convenient to come every day to Christ as a sinner— as I came at first. "You are no saint," says the devil. Well, if I am not, I am a sinner, and Jesus Christ came into the world to save sinners. Sink or swim, there I go—other hope I have none.

Peace By Believing,
Volume 9, Sermon #510 - Romans 5:1

True religion is something more than correct opinions. A man may as well descend to hell being orthodox as heterodox.

The Faculty Baffled, the Great Physical Successful,
Volume 14, Sermon #827 - Mark 5:25-28

I will tell you one thing,—if you believe in Jesus Christ and you are damned, I will be damned with you.

Aeneas,
Volume 22, Sermon #1315 - Acts 9:32-35

To convince men of the truth of a statement is one thing, to convince them of personal sin is another thing, and to convert them is a step higher still.

God's Work Upon Minister and Convert,
Volume 30, Sermon #1774 - Acts 26:16-20

Though no man is free from the commission of sin, yet every converted man is free from the love of sin.

Two Essential Things,
Volume 35, Sermon #2073 - Acts 20:21

That conversion which is all joy and lacks sorrow for sin, is very questionable.

Two Essential Things,
Volume 35, Sermon #2073 - Acts 20:21

There is no real salvation except salvation from sinning, so your sin must be quitted.

Why Some Seekers Are Not Saved,
Volume 41, Sermon #2411 - Isaiah 59:1, 2

This is a miracle; it is as much a work of God to make us children of light as it was to make light at the first.

Despised Light Withdrawn,
Volume 41, Sermon #2413 - John 12:36

Christ will not blot out your sins in the past, unless you are willing to be cured of the love of sin in the present, and the pursuit of sin in the future.

Christ's Triple Character,
Volume 48, Sermon #2787 - Isaiah 55:4

I know that emotion does not save the soul, but I believe that those who are saved are usually filled with emotion.

The Seed Upon A Rock,
Volume 49, Sermon #2844 - Matthew 13:5, 6

This is how God saves men—by leading them to trust in Him in Jesus Christ.

The Life-Lock,
Volume 50, Sermon #2867 - Isaiah 45:22

We are not saved by faith itself as a meritorious work. There is no merit in believing in God and even if there were, it could not save us, since salvation by merit has been once and for all solemnly excluded.

The Search Warrant,
Volume 50, Sermon #2898 - John 6:64

I used to think that believing in Christ was some mysterious thing and I could not make out what it was—but when I heard that it was just this— "Look unto Me, and be you saved," I found that the only reason why it was so hard was that it was so easy!

The Search Warrant,
Volume 50, Sermon #2898 - John 6:64

No matter how far off a man may be from God, if there is a hearty and earnest seeking after Him through Jesus Christ, he will find Him.

Reasons for Doubting Christ,
Volume 51, Sermon #2925 - Matthew 14:31

I know this, if the Lord had not first loved me, I never would have loved Him. And if there is any good thing in men whatever, it must have been implanted there by the Holy Spirit. If salvation is of works, then I can never have it—and if it is the reward of natural goodness, then I shall never have it. I feel that it must be of Grace, and of Grace alone.

Stephen and Saul,
Volume 51, Sermon #2948 - Acts 7:58

If you are to be saved by your own works, you must be absolutely perfect, in thought, and word, and deed, from the moment of your birth to the hour of your death.

The Two Debtors,
Volume 52, Sermon #3015 - Luke 7:41, 42

The work of God in the soul is a lasting and an everlasting work! If you are once healed by Christ, He has worked in you an effectual cure which will hold good throughout time and throughout eternity!

Good Cheer from Grace Received,
Volume 53, Sermon #3020 - Matthew 9:20-22, Luke 8:42-48

If you really desire to have Christ's love shed abroad in your heart,that is a proof that Christ has already fixed His love upon you! If your head is now beaten upon by the fierce sunlight of God's wrath, you may come and find a shelter in the great rock of Christ's atoning Sacrifice!

"The Shadow of A Great Rock",
Volume 53, Sermon #3031 - Isaiah 32:3

"Oh, what amazing mercy," each saved soul may well say, "and all this for me!" Everlasting love ordained it, immutable love has accomplished it, and unchanging love will perfect it.

"Going and Weeping",
Volume 53, Sermon #3049 - Jeremiah 50:4

If you cannot be perfect, God will not save you by works.

Christ's Prayer for Believers,
Volume 55, Sermon #3133 - John 17:20

You will be saved, not by repenting and tears! Not by wailing and works! Not by doing and praying, but coming, believing, simply depending upon what Jesus Christ has done! When your soul says by faith what Christ said in fact, "It is finished," you are saved and you may go your way rejoicing!

The True Aim of Preaching,
Volume 56, Sermon #3191 - Acts 13:38

Surely the Lord does not create life in the regenerated soul without providing stores upon which it may be nourished! Where He gives life, He gives food.

How the Lambs Feed,
Volume 56, Sermon #3199 - Isaiah 5:17

Why did God send a Savior if you need no saving?

The Sealed Hand—A Winter Sermon,
Volume 58, Sermon #3289 - Job 37:7

You may work your fingers to the bone, but you can never weave a righteousness that shall cover your nakedness before God.

"The Blood of the Testament",
Volume 58, Sermon #3293 - Hebrews 9:19, 20

It is not enough for us to say, "I believe in the Lord Jesus Christ and, therefore, I am saved." That is not the end of it all, otherwise religion were a grand piece of selfishness!

A Practical Discourse,
Volume 58, Sermon #3313 - 1 Kings 5:14

The only salvation that can redeem from Hell is a salvation which comes from Heaven! Eternal salvation must come from an eternal God. Salvation that makes you a new creature must be the work of Him who sits upon the Throne of God and makes all things new!

God in Heaven, and Men on the Sea,
Volume 58, Sermon #3321 - Psalm 65:5

Like Jonah, you may lose your gourd, but you cannot lose your God.

Two Choice Benedictions,
Volume 59, Sermon #3371 - Numbers 6:23-27, 2 Corinthians 13:14

Salvation is, in short, deliverance from sin, deliverance from the guilt of it, from the punishment of it, from the power of it.

Right-Hand Sins,
Volume 60, Sermon #3415 - Mark 9:43

None are excluded hence but those who do themselves exclude.

A Solemn Embassy,
Volume 62, Sermon #3497 - 2 Corinthians 5:20

Sanctification

The truth is the sanctifier, and if we do not hear or read the truth, we shall not grow in sanctification. We only progress in sound living as we progress in sound understanding.

Morning and Evening, Page 372

The most golden faith or the purest degree of sanctification to which a Christian ever attained on earth, has still so much alloy in it as to be only worthy of the flames, in itself considered.

Morning and Evening, Page 603

He has come to deliver us, not from you, O death, alone! nor from you, O hell, alone! but from you, O sin, the mother of death, the progenitor of hell!

Messers. Moody and Sankey Defended,
Volume 21, Sermon #1239 - Galatians 5:24

He that is saved continues to be saved, and goes on to be saved from day to day, from every sin and from every form of evil.

A Summary of Experience and a Body of Divinity,
Volume 30, Sermon #1806 - 1 Thessalonians 1:9, 10

Every truth leads towards holiness; every error of doctrine, directly or indirectly, leads to sin.

Our Lord's Prayer for His People's Sanctification,
Volume 32, Sermon #1890 - John 17:17

Albeit sanctification is the work of the Holy Spirit, yet it is equally true, and this we must ever bear in mind, that the Holy Spirit makes us active agents in our own sanctification.

Our Position and Our Purpose,
Volume 57, Sermon #3245 - 2 Corinthians 7:1

I can imagine a room in your house being perfectly clean, but I cannot imagine its being kept perfectly clean unless the process by which it was first cleansed be frequently repeated.

Our Position and Our Purpose,
Volume 57, Sermon #3245 - 2 Corinthians 7:1

Satan

He wriggles about like a serpent, but he cannot rule like a sovereign.

Faith's Checkbook, Page 211

Satan has cunning servants about him, that hunt for the precious life with double diligence.

A Good Start, Page 259

He can never be content till he sees the believer utterly devoured. He would rend him in pieces, and break his bones, and utterly destroy him, if he could. Do not, therefore, indulge the thought, that the main purpose of Satan is to make you miserable.

The Roaring Lion,
Volume 7, Sermon #419 - 1 Peter 5:8, 9

There is something, however, very comforting in the thought that he is an adversary: I would sooner have him for an adversary than for a friend. O my soul, it were dread work with me if Satan were a friend of mine, for then with him you must for ever dwell in darkness and in the deeps, shut out from the friendship of God; but to have Satan for an adversary is a comfortable omen, for it looks as if God were our friend, and so far let us be comforted in this matter.

Zechariah's Vision of Joshua the High Priest,
Volume 11, Sermon #611 - Zechariah 3:1-5

Satan does not care whether he drags you down to hell as a Calvinist or as an Arminian, so long as he can get you there.

Kicking Against the Pricks,
Volume 12, Sermon #709 - Acts 9:5

Satan will be glad if you begin to blame the preacher when you ought to have blamed yourself.

Kicking Against the Pricks,
Volume 12, Sermon #709 - Acts 9:5

Satan knows right well that one devil in the church can do far more than a thousand devils outside her bounds.

Spots in Our Feasts of Charity,
Volume 14, Sermon #797 - Jude 1:12

Sin is worse than the devil, since it made the devil what he is. Satan as an existence is God's creature, and sin never was; its origin and nature are altogether apart from God.

The Monster Dragged to Light,
Volume 19, Sermon #1095 - Romans 7:13

I question whether anyone is more orthodox than the devil; for the devils believe and tremble. Satan is no sceptic; he has too much knowledge for that.

The Horns of the Altar,
Volume 31, Sermon #1826 - 1 Kings 2:30

While you are sleeping, Satan will be sowing.

The Sluggard's Farm,
Volume 34, Sermon #2027 - Proverbs 23:30-32

The trail of the old serpent is everywhere.

"Blessed in Him",
Volume 42, Sermon #2451 - Psalm 72:17

Why, the devil never puts an "if" to anything that is not true; whenever he says "if" to a thing, we may be sure that it is true.

Sonship Questioned,
Volume 45, Sermon #2613 - Matthew 4:3

He is always watching to see where you are not looking; he is always on the alert when you are slumbering.

An Antidote to Satan's Devices,
Volume 46, Sermon #2707 - Genesis 3:1

We had better go a thousand miles, over hedge and ditch, than have to stand foot to foot with that dread adversary of our souls for an hour.

Lame Sheep,
Volume 49, Sermon #2854 - Hebrews 12:13

That "to-morrow" plea is a false one. Satan has invented it in order that he may enable men to reject Christ, and yet flatter their souls with the notion that they are not doing so.

"To You",
Volume 50, Sermon #2899 - Acts 13:26

Only Satan himself could have put it into a man's heart to become a salaried preacher of the gospel in order to deny its fundamental truths.

Beauty for Ashes,
Volume 59, Sermon #3336 - Isaiah 61:3

Sayings

Our motto is, "with God, anywhere: without God, nowhere."

Barbed Arrows, Page 182

When the Lord Jesus loves a man very much, He gives him much to do or much to suffer.

Come Ye Children, Page 55

In the case of every errant course there is always a first wrong step.

The Down Grade Controversy, Page 13

Do not be satisfied with the practice without the principles of piety.

A Good Start, Page 167

Life is made up of little incidents, and success in it often depends upon attention to minor details.

Lectures to My Students,
Volume 2, Page 96

The more spiritual the exercise, the sooner we tire in it.

Morning and Evening, Page 49

Vain pursuits are dangerous to unrenewed souls.

Morning and Evening, Page 331

Jesus, be mine for ever, my God, my heaven, my all.

Morning and Evening, Page 335

May your convictions be deep, your love real, your desires earnest.

Morning and Evening, Page 386

Nothing teaches us so much the preciousness of the Creator, as when we learn the emptiness of all besides.

Morning and Evening, Page 649

Pangs go with birth, and anguish precedes success.

Only A Prayer Meeting, Page 41

It is never worthwhile to do unnecessary things.

John Ploughman's Pictures, Page 71

Slow and sure is better than fast and flimsy.

John Ploughman's Talk, Page 138

Earn all you can, save all you can, and then give all you can.

John Ploughman's Talk, Page 147

I am descended from the King of kings.

Words of Cheer, Page 29

Men will allow God to be everywhere except on his throne.

Divine Sovereignty,
Volume 2, Sermon #77 - Matthew 20:15

No man has anything of his own, except his sins.

The Two Talents,
Volume 4, Sermon #175 - Matthew 25:22, 23

Human nature does not mind what you tell it to do, so long as you do not tell it to believe.

The Form and Spirit of Religion,
Volume 4, Sermon #186 - 1 Samuel 4:3

Most men would be very religious if religion did not entail obligations.

A Present Religion,
Volume 4, Sermon #196 - 1 John 3:2

Now, it is not likely that the God who made a happy world would send a miserable salvation.

A Free Salvation,
Volume 4, Sermon #199 - Isaiah 55:1

Has there not been, sometimes, this temptation to do a great deal for Christ, but not to live a great deal with Christ?

Declension from First Love,
Volume 4, Sermon #217 - Revelation 2:4

Time, how short—eternity, how long! Death, how brief—immortality, how endless!

Prayer Answered, Love Nourished,
Volume 5, Sermon #240 - Psalm 116:1

The men that escape without abuse in this world, are the men who do nothing at all.

The Best of Masters,
Volume 5, Sermon #247 - John 14:27

When men have no faith, God invites them to reason, but when they have faith, reasoning with God becomes a sin.

The Call of Abraham,
Volume 5, Sermon #261 - Hebrews 11:8

Man is always altering what God has ordained. Although God's order is ever the best, yet man will never agree therewith.

Limiting God,
Volume 5, Sermon #272 - Psalm 78:41

Devils are not to be reasoned with, but to be cast out.

A Blow at Self-Righteousness,
Volume 7, Sermon #350 - Job 9:20

Never stain one duty with the blood of another.

A Sermon for the Week of Prayer,
Volume 7, Sermon #354 - Colossians 4:2

I would never believe that we were on the Lord's side if all men were on our side.

The Earnest of Heaven,
Volume 7, Sermon #358 - Ephesians 1:13, 14

Begin at the bottom, and grow up; but do not begin at the top, and come down.

The Interest of Christ and His People in Each Other,
Volume 7, Sermon #374 - Song of Solomon 2:16

If the great enemy, Sin, has been conquered, we shall not fear the little enemy, Death.

Perfect Cleansing,
Volume 7, Sermon #379 - Joel 3:21

I believe the perfection of the Wesleyan is nothing more than the justification of a Calvinist.

Perfect Cleansing,
Volume 7, Sermon #379 - Joel 3:21

"Difficult," said Napoleon, "is not a French word." "Doubtful," is not a Christian word.

The Missionaries' Charge and Charter,
Volume 7, Sermon #383 - Matthew 28:18, 19

Do what you believe to be right, and ever hold it for a maxim, that if the skies fall through your doing right, honest men will survive the ruin.

Trust in God—True Wisdom,
Volume 7, Sermon #392 - Proverbs 16:20

Thy first birth gave you life and death together.

The New Nature,
Volume 7, Sermon #398 - 1 Peter 1:23-25

Men hate hell for the reason that murderers hate the gallows.

Not Now, But Hereafter!,
Volume 7, Sermon #410 - Job 21:29-31

It is human to err, it is divine to repent.

God's First Words to the First Sinner,
Volume 7, Sermon #412 - Genesis 3:9

One of the greatest mercies God bestows upon us is his not permitting our inclinations and opportunities to meet.

The Roaring Lion,
Volume 7, Sermon #419 - 1 Peter 5:8, 9

It is only serving God that is doing immortal work; it is only living for Christ that is living at all.

Life in Earnest,
Volume 8, Sermon #433 - 2 Chronicles 31:21

The rending of the veil of death is the removal of much of our ignorance.

The Elders Before the Throne,
Volume 8, Sermon #441 - Revelation 4:4; 10, 11

The more holy, the more humble.

The Elders Before the Throne,
Volume 8, Sermon #441 - Revelation 4:4; 10, 11

It would be infinitely better to bury you in the earth than see you buried in sin.

Enduring to the End,
Volume 10, Sermon #554 - Matthew 10:22

There is an orthodox as well as a heterodox road to hell, and the devil knows how to handle Calvinists quite as well as Arminians.

Nothing But Leaves,
Volume 10, Sermon #555 - Mark 11:13

You cannot have Christ in eternity if you do not have him in time.

A Bundle of Myrrh,
Volume 10, Sermon #558 - Song of Solomon 1:13

Prevention is better than a cure, and sometimes a timely heart-searching may save us many a heart-smarting.

The Barley Field on Fire,
Volume 10, Sermon #563 - 2 Samuel 14:29-31

Very well, Christian, be content to be behind the times, for the times are getting nearer to judgment and the last plagues.

"Let Us Go forth",
Volume 10, Sermon #577 - Hebrews 13:13

Death is a great revealer of secrets.

An Awful Premonition,
Volume 10, Sermon #594 - Matthew 16:28

It were infinitely better that the Christian should pay too much than too little. He had better be blamed for an excess of generosity, than take credit to himself for a rigid parsimony.

The Centurion,
Volume 10, Sermon #600 - Luke 7:4-9

Shake the foundations upon which the eternity of hell rests, and you have shaken heaven's eternity too.

The Smoke of Their Torments,
Volume 10, Sermon #602 - Genesis 19:27, 28

I live in Jesus, on Jesus, with Jesus, and soon hope to be perfectly conformed to his likeness.

Now,
Volume 10, Sermon #603 - 2 Corinthians 6:2

Be not like those who dream of a God who is all love, and nothing else.

Knowledge Commended,
Volume 11, Sermon #609 - Daniel 11:32, 33

The best of men are still men at the best.

Sweet Savor,
Volume 12, Sermon #688 - Ezekiel 20:41

He judges his Judge, and misjudges.

Let Not Your Heart Be Troubled,
Volume 13, Sermon #730 - John 14:1

A Christian's experience is like a rainbow, made up of drops of the grief of earth, and beams of the bliss of heaven.

Creation's Groans and the Saint's Sighs,
Volume 14, Sermon #788 - Romans 8:22, 23

Where persons love little, do little, and give little, we may shrewdly suspect that they have never had much affliction of heart for their sins and that they think they owe but very little to divine grace.

Mary Magdalene,
Volume 14, Sermon #792 - Mark 16:9

We are not what we might be, we are not what we should be, we are not what we shall be, we are not what we wish to be.

Nearer and Dearer,
Volume 14, Sermon #793 - Song of Solomon 5:2-8

We commonly say that "there is no rule without an exception," and certainly the rule that there is no rule without an exception has an exception to itself, for the rules of God are without exception.

Noah's Flood,
Volume 14, Sermon #823 - Matthew 24:39

To be just alive as a Christian is horrid work.

Ripe Fruit,
Volume 16, Sermon #945 - Micah 7:1

I would be nothing but what he makes me, I would have nothing but what he gives me, I would ask nothing but what he promises me, I would trust in nothing but what he has done for me, and I would desire nothing but what he has prepared for me.

The One Thing Needful,
Volume 17, Sermon #1015 - Luke 10:42

Beloved, our crusty tempers and sour faces will never be evangelists.

Always and for All Things,
Volume 19, Sermon #1094 - Ephesians 5:20

I suppose we may judge of a man more by that wherein he finds his pleasure than by almost anything else.

"The Lord Is Risen, Indeed",
Volume 19, Sermon #1106 - Luke 24:5, 6

The moment a man says, "I have it," he will no longer try to obtain it; the moment he cries, "It is enough," he will not labour after more.

Onward!,
Volume 19, Sermon #1114 - Philippians 3:13, 14

When we mix with dwarfs we think ourselves giants, but in the presence of giants we become dwarfs.

Onward!,
Volume 19, Sermon #1114 - Philippians 3:13, 14

We live too fast by half, we do too much and accomplish, therefore, too little.

Medicine for the Distracted,
Volume 19, Sermon #1116 - Psalm 94:19

We have left the miry clay for the solid rock.

Paved with Love,
Volume 19, Sermon #1134 - Song of Solomon 3:10

Madness has been prevented by the soul's finding vent.

Consolation for the Despairing,
Volume 19, Sermon #1146 - Psalm 31:22

Consequences and usefulness are nothing to us: duty and right—these are to be our guides.

Daniel Facing The Lion's Den,
Volume 20, Sermon #1154 - Daniel 6:10

The man who does not forgive has never been forgiven, but the man who has been freely forgiven at once forgives others.

Without Money and Without Price,
Volume 20, Sermon #1161 - Isaiah 55:1

What a man is at home, that he is, and though he be a saint abroad, if he be a devil at home, you may depend upon it that the last is his real character.

The Christian's Motto,
Volume 20, Sermon #1165 - John 8:29

What would you do if you might be indulged? because whatever you would do if you had your own way, is the test of your heart.

The Christian's Motto,
Volume 20, Sermon #1165 - John 8:29

A people are in an evil case when all their heroism is historical.

The Fullness of Christ the Treasury of the Saints,
Volume 20, Sermon #1169 - Colossians 1:19, John 1:16

Expecting great things, let us attempt great things.

The Fullness of Christ the Treasury of the Saints,
Volume 20, Sermon #1169 - Colossians 1:19, John 1:16

I know of nothing which makes a man so grossly vicious as to be persuaded that virtue is impossible to him.

Thinking and Turning,
Volume 20, Sermon #1181 - Psalm 119:59

Hell has many gates, though heaven has but one.

Thinking and Turning,
Volume 20, Sermon #1181 - Psalm 119:59

While carnal men say "seeing is believing," we assure them that to us "believing is seeing."

A Singular Title and a Special Favor,
Volume 20, Sermon #1182 - Psalm 59:10

A convert once said, "Either the world is altered or else I am."

Is Conversion Necessary?,
Volume 20, Sermon #1183 - 2 Corinthians 5:17

Nothing seems to be too foolish, nothing too wicked, nothing too insane, for mankind.

The Sad Plight and Sure Relief,
Volume 20, Sermon #1184 - Romans 5:6

We gain nothing by the love of those that love not God.

A Word for the Persecuted,
Volume 20, Sermon #1188 - 1 Samuel 20:10

You are as ready at forgetting as you are at resolving.

The Turning Point,
Volume 20, Sermon #1189 - Luke 15:20

If you want a thing well done, you must go to the man who has a great deal to do, for he is the man to do it for you.

Hindrances to Prayer,
Volume 20, Sermon #1192 - 1 Peter 3:7

They say of some that they are as easy as an old shoe, and they are generally worth no more than that article.

Hindrances to Prayer,
Volume 20, Sermon #1192 - 1 Peter 3:7

You cannot trust God too much, nor trust yourself too little.

Girding On the Harness,
Volume 20, Sermon #1193 - 1 Kings 20:11

Do not try to be a wonder, but be a wonder.

"I and the Children",
Volume 20, Sermon #1194 - Isaiah 8:18

To a man who lives unto God nothing is secular, everything is sacred.

Heart-Knowledge of God,
Volume 20, Sermon #1206 - Jeremiah 24:7

Half the mischief in the world, and perhaps more, is done, not by an ostensible lie, but by a perverted truth.

Infallibility—Where to Find It and How to Use It,
Volume 20, Sermon #1208 - Matthew 4:4

It will be found much easier to go down from God to nature when you once know the Lord than ever it can be to ascend from the works to the Maker.

A God Ready to Pardon,
Volume 22, Sermon #1272 - Nehemiah 9:17

The stool of repentance and the foot of the cross are the favorite positions of instructed Christians.

Unconditional Surrender,
Volume 22, Sermon #1276 - James 4:7

After all, my friend, to tell you the truth very plainly, you are no better than other people, though you think you are, and in one point I am sure you miserably fail, and that is in humility.

Life's Need and Maintenance,
Volume 22, Sermon #1300 - Psalm 22:29

"I have set the Lord always before me." Refuse to see anything without seeing God in it.

The Secret of a Happy Life,
Volume 22, Sermon #1305 - Psalm 16:8

To sin because of mercy is a step lower than even the devil has descended.

A Second Word to Seekers,
Volume 22, Sermon #1313 - Jeremiah 29:13

To weep over a dying Savior is to lament the remedy; it were wiser to bewail the disease.

Why Should I Weep?,
Volume 22, Sermon #1320 - Luke 23:27-31

Right is right though all condemn, and wrong is wrong though all approve.

Sins of Ignorance,
Volume 23, Sermon #1386 - Leviticus 5:17, 18

A thousand ages of whitewashing cannot make a vice a virtue.

Sins of Ignorance,
Volume 23, Sermon #1386 - Leviticus 5:17, 18

Party leaders are sure to be found where there is a party spirit; and party spirit is a fungus which grows upon the dunghill of conceit.

A Catechism for the Proud,
Volume 24, Sermon #1392 - 1 Corinthians 4:7

In estimating our personal character, let us not so much calculate what we could be, as what we are.

A Catechism for the Proud,
Volume 24, Sermon #1392 - 1 Corinthians 4:7

It is an easy way to save your skin, to believe what you believe and let other people alone.

God's Advocates Breaking Silence,
Volume 24, Sermon #1403 - Job 36:2

A big heart is one of the main essentials to great usefulness.

Compassion on the Ignorant,
Volume 24, Sermon #1407 - Hebrews 5:2

I am sure it is so: that which costs us most we value most.

Compassion on the Ignorant,
Volume 24, Sermon #1407 - Hebrews 5:2

The increase of the burden is not the thing to groan about if there be a proportionate increase of strength.

A Sacred Solo,
Volume 24, Sermon #1423 - Psalm 28:7

To my mind there is hardly anything more sad than the frequent laughter which exposes a vacant mind.

A Sacred Solo,
Volume 24, Sermon #1423 - Psalm 28:7

The full he empties, and the empty he fills.

A Woman of a Sorrowful Spirit,
Volume 26, Sermon #1515 - 1 Samuel 1:15

Henceforth be devotion your breathing, faith your heartbeat, meditation your feeding, self-examination your washing, and holiness your walking.

The Devil's Last Throw,
Volume 29, Sermon #1746 - Luke 9:42

Men have been helped to live by remembering that they must

die; yea, some men knew nothing of the highest form of life till death aroused them from their deadly slumbers.

What Is Your Life?,
Volume 30, Sermon #1773 - James 4:14

O brethren, everything is right when the heart is right, and everything is wrong when the soul is wrong.

Grappling Irons,
Volume 30, Sermon #1779 - Psalm 119:88

God is dearest when goods are fewest. Heaven is warmest when earth is coldest.

A Sweet Silver Bell Ringing in Each Believer's Heart,
Volume 31, Sermon #1819 - Micah 7:7

We are great at calculations when we are little at believing.

Certain Curious Calculations about Loaves and Fishes,
Volume 31, Sermon #1822 - Mark 8:19-21

To believe him that cannot lie, and trust in him that cannot fail, is a kind of wisdom that none but fools will laugh at.

Elijah's Plea,
Volume 31, Sermon #1832 - 1 Kings 18:36

Even the best of believers are not always at their best.

A Proclamation from the King of Kings,
Volume 31, Sermon #1833 - Jeremiah 3:12, 13

We are afraid of the razor which cuts too close to the skin.

The Private Tutor,
Volume 31, Sermon #1842 - John 14:24-26

The dust of earth has blinded eyes that were meant for heaven.

A Traitor Suspected and Convicted,
Volume 32, Sermon #1878 - Romans 8:7

I know that I have no perfection in my best things, much less in my worst.

A Plain Man's Sermon,
Volume 32, Sermon #1879 - Leviticus 22:21

He who would please all attempts the impossible. God himself is quarreled with.

Retrospect—"The Lord Has Blessed",
Volume 32, Sermon #1882 - Joshua 17:14

Success comes not to heartless efforts.

Exhortation—"Set Your Heart",
Volume 32, Sermon #1884 - 1 Chronicles 22:19

The Christian man who does not give God the morning of his days is not very likely to give him much of the evening.

Exhortation—"Set Your Heart",
Volume 32, Sermon #1884 - 1 Chronicles 22:19

We are not the world's, else might we be ambitious; we are not Satan's, else might we be covetous; we are not our own, else might we be selfish.

Our Lord's Prayer for His People's Sanctification,
Volume 32, Sermon #1890 - John 17:17

The seed of the woman knows no terms with the serpent brood but continual war.

Our Lord's Prayer for His People's Sanctification,
Volume 32, Sermon #1890 - John 17:17

The straight line of truth drawn on the heart will produce a direct course of gracious walking in the life.

Our Lord's Prayer for His People's Sanctification,
Volume 32, Sermon #1890 - John 17:17

The uncertainty of the end of all things is intended to keep us continually on the watch.

The Sermon of the Seasons,
Volume 32, Sermon #1891 - Genesis 8:22

Where there is life there must be change; only in death is there monotony.

The Sermon of the Seasons,
Volume 32, Sermon #1891 - Genesis 8:22

Behind us is our trust; before us is our hope.

The Two Appearing and the Discipline of Grace,
Volume 32, Sermon #1894 - Titus 2:11-14

Things which men call absurdities have become foundation truths to us.

The Three Hours of Darkness,
Volume 32, Sermon #1896 - Matthew 27:45

If we get to think that everything must be big to be good, we shall get into a sorry state of mind.

Mysterious Meat,
Volume 32, Sermon #1901 - John 4:31-38

If we never do any work for Christ except when we feel up to the mark, we shall not do much.

How to Become Fishers of Men,
Volume 32, Sermon #1906 - Matthew 4:19

Be not influenced by those who cry loudest in the street, or by those who beat the biggest drum.

A Seasonable Exhortation,
Volume 32, Sermon #1909 - 1 Peter 1:13

How often have I wished that I could forget many things which once I thought it necessary to know.

The Holy Road,
Volume 32, Sermon #1912

God grant that we may never stretch the arm of our testimony beyond the sleeve of our experience!

The Holy Road,
Volume 32, Sermon #1912

One hair from the head of love will draw more than the cable of fear.

Secret Drawings Graciously Explained,
Volume 32, Sermon #1914 - Jeremiah 31:3

It is no joy to see a harvest reaped from fields which we refused to plough.

The Great Sin of Doing Nothing,
Volume 32, Sermon #1916 - Numbers 32:23

He that is ashamed to speak the truth has need to be ashamed of himself.

The Very Bold Prophecy,
Volume 32, Sermon #1919 - Isaiah 65:1

If men do not find God they have found nothing.

The Very Bold Prophecy,
Volume 32, Sermon #1919 - Isaiah 65:1

God is the sum of our necessities.

The Very Bold Prophecy,
Volume 32, Sermon #1919 - Isaiah 65:1

Beloved friends, we live in a world of sin and sorrow, and we ourselves are sinful and sorrowful; we need one who can put away our sin and become a sharer in our sorrow.

Our Sympathizing High Priest,
Volume 32, Sermon #1927 - Hebrews 5:7-10

You will not always be able to travel to heaven in secret.

Is It True?,
Volume 32, Sermon #1930 - Daniel 3:14

How much of external religion is fiction, fluff, form, foam!

Is It True?,
Volume 32, Sermon #1930 - Daniel 3:14

He loves not Christ who does not love him more than all things.

Is It True?,
Volume 32, Sermon #1930 - Daniel 3:14

If men are not warned of the anger of God against iniquity, they will take license to riot in evil.

One More Cast of the Great Net,
Volume 32, Sermon #1931 - Joel 2:32

The difficulties of unbelief are ten times greater than the difficulties of faith.

Driving the Vultures Away from the Sacrifice,
Volume 33, Sermon #1993 - Genesis 15:11

Ah, it is better to lay one brick to-day than to propose to build a palace next year!

"Where Are the Nine?"—Or, Praise Neglected,
Volume 32, Sermon #1935 - Luke 17:15-19

I would rather be nobody at Christ's feet than everybody anywhere else!

"Where Are the Nine?"-Or, Praise Neglected,
Volume 32, Sermon #1935 - Luke 17:15-19

There is no use in having a God if you do not use him.

The Master Key—Opening the Gate of Heaven,
Volume 33, Sermon #1938 - Genesis 32:12

Nothing can happen but what God ordains; and, therefore, why should we fear?

Earthquake But Not Heartquake,
Volume 33, Sermon #1950 - Psalm 46:1-3

The man who begins to exult over his fallen brother is the likeliest man to fall himself.

A Testimony to Free and Sovereign Grace,
Volume 33, Sermon #1953 - Psalm 37:39

If the present contest should be continued century after century, be not weary. It is only long to your impatience; it is a short work unto God.

The Search for Faith,
Volume 33, Sermon #1963 - Luke 18:8

Let us crush the eggs of our woes while they lie in the nest of our unbelief. Our sorrows are mostly manufactured at home, beaten out upon the anvil of unbelief with the hammer of our foreboding.

Why Is Faith So Feeble?,
Volume 33, Sermon #1964 - Mark 4:40

Brethren, we are never so weak as when we feel strongest, and never so foolish as when we dream that we are wise.

Why Is Faith So Feeble?,
Volume 33, Sermon #1964 - Mark 4:40

We shall never go right unless God is first, midst, and last.

A Bit of History for Old and Young,
Volume 33, Sermon #1972 - Genesis 48:16, 16

On earth he bleeds, in heaven he pleads.

Trust,
Volume 33, Sermon #1978 - Ephesians 1:12, 13

All your wants his love has supplied: there are shoes for your pilgrimage, armor for your warfare, strength for your labour, rest for your weariness, comfort for your sorrow.

Love At Its Utmost,
Volume 33, Sermon #1982 - John 15:9

That we live is miraculous; that we die is but natural.

Man, Whose Breath Is in His Nostrils,
Volume 33, Sermon #1984 - Isaiah 2:22

What a sad world man has made this earth!

Song for the Free—Hope for the Bound,
Volume 33, Sermon #1992 - Psalm 107:14-16

Your goods shall be your good, if you learn to use them for God's glory.

The Lover of God's Law Filled with Peace,
Volume 34, Sermon #2004 - Psalm 119:165

Few of us are perfectly sane. In fact, I do not think anybody is altogether so.

Nathanael-Or, the Ready Believer and His Reward,
Volume 34, Sermon #2021 - John 1:50

Men will do little for what they doubt, and much for what they believe.

The Blessing of Full Assurance,
Volume 34, Sermon #2023 - 1 John 5:13

To enter into debate is never as profitable as to enter into devotion.

Plain Directions to Those Who Would Be Saved from Sin,
Volume 34, Sermon #2033 - Psalm 4:4, 5

Life is long enough if we have had grace enough.

Crossing the Jordan,
Volume 34, Sermon #2039 - Joshua 1:10, 11

Evil things are easy things: for they are natural to our fallen nature.
Right things are rare flowers that need cultivation.

Sown Among Thorns,
Volume 34, Sermon #2040 - Matthew 13:7, 22

Pleasure so called is the murderer of thought.

Sown Among Thorns,
Volume 34, Sermon #2040 - Matthew 13:7, 22

Truth is of necessity intolerant of error.

Jesus Known by Personal Revelation,
Volume 34, Sermon #2041 - Matthew 16:13-17

Do you think of turning back? You have no armor for your back.
To cease to fight is to be overcome.

The Blood of the Lamb, The Conquering Weapon,
Volume 34, Sermon #2043 - Revelation 12:11

The idle are troublesome; the laborious are loving.

All At It,
Volume 34, Sermon #2044 - Acts 8:4, 5, 35

Unless the Lord renews the heart, men will always prefer the bird-
in-the-hand of this life to the bird-in-the-bush of the life to come.

No Compromise,
Volume 34, Sermon #2047 - Genesis 24:5-8

It is well to be nothing: it is better still to be "less than nothing."

A Paradox,
Volume 34, Sermon #2050 - 2 Corinthians 12:10

Sufferers are our tutors; they educate us for the skies.

The Trial of Your Faith,
Volume 34, Sermon #2055 - 1 Peter 1:7

The first movement is from God to us, not from us to God.

The Lord's Own Salvation,
Volume 34, Sermon #2057 - Hosea 1:7

Some of us might have enjoyed a much larger blessing, if we had not grown top-heavy with the blessing we already enjoyed.

The Lord's Own Salvation,
Volume 34, Sermon #2057 - Hosea 1:7

Have something to do, and do it. Have something to live for, and live for it.

"Eyes Right",
Volume 34, Sermon #2058 - Proverbs 4:25

Too many wound themselves by studying themselves.

"Eyes Right",
Volume 34, Sermon #2058 - Proverbs 4:25

No man does a thing well who does it sorrowfully.

Our Great Shepherd Finding the Sheep,
Volume 35, Sermon #2065 - Luke 15:4, 5, 6

Certain people must always have sweets and comforts; but God's wise children do not wish for these in undue measure. Daily bread we ask for, not daily sugar.

Trembling At the Word of the Lord,
Volume 35, Sermon #2071 - Isaiah 66:2

He who seeks comfort at the expense of truth will be a fool for his pains.

Trembling At the Word of the Lord,
Volume 35, Sermon #2071 - Isaiah 66:2

The voices of earth are full of falsehood, but the word from heaven is very pure.

The Bible Tried and Proved,
Volume 35, Sermon #2084 - Psalm 12:6

The course of our fallen race has been a succession of failures.

Grace for Grace,
Volume 35, Sermon #2087 - 1 Corinthians 2:12

If you have no wish to bring others to heaven, you are not going there yourself.

Grace for Grace,
Volume 35, Sermon #2087 - 1 Corinthians 2:12

Grace does not run in the blood.

The form of Godliness Without the Power,
Volume 35, Sermon #2089

God has given you a nature that wars against evil: hence these tears!

Concerning the Consolations of God,
Volume 35, Sermon #2099 - Job 15:11

Better suffer anything than do wrong.

Concerning the Consolations of God,
Volume 35, Sermon #2099 - Job 15:11

Wealth brings care, honor earns envy, position entails toil, and rank has its annoyances.

Concerning the Consolations of God,
Volume 35, Sermon #2099 - Job 15:11

To attempt a difficulty may be laudable, but to rush upon an impossibility is madness.

Faith Essential to Pleasing God,
Volume 35, Sermon #2100 - Hebrews 11:6

One single individual can scatter benedictions across a continent, and belt the world with blessing.

The Mustard Seed-A Sermon for the Sunday School Teacher,
Volume 35, Sermon #2110 - Luke 13:18-19

Some are never pleased with God; how can he be pleased with them?

Peace-How Gained, How Broken,
Volume 35, Sermon #2112 - Psalm 85:8

Oh, for that godliness which will strengthen you to quit your situation, to lose your wealth, to sacrifice your credit, and to part with your friends sooner than grieve your Lord!

By the Fountain,
Volume 35, Sermon #2113 - Genesis 49:22, Deuteronomy 32:13

We need to grow thus healthily independent of human judgment; for he who fawns for smiles, or trembles at frowns, will never lead a noble life for long.

The Planter of the Ear Must Hear,
Volume 35, Sermon #2118 - Psalm 94:9

Man's security is the devil's opportunity.

The Keynote of the Year,
Volume 36, Sermon #2121 - Psalm 103:1

Many a child of God has to weep for months because he did not watch for minutes.

Hope for Your Future,
Volume 36, Sermon #2125 - Ezekiel 36:11

Bible-reading people seldom go off to modern theology.

The Warnings and the Rewards of the Word of God,
Volume 36, Sermon #2135 - Psalm 19:11

One mark of a man's true wisdom is his knowledge of his ignorance.

A Homily for Humble Folks,
Volume 36, Sermon #2140 - Proverbs 30:2

If you can do but little, make the best of yourself by intensity.

A Homily for Humble Folks,
Volume 36, Sermon #2140 - Proverbs 30:2

He who does not believe that God will cast unbelievers into hell, will not be sure that he will take believers to heaven.

Noah's Faith, Fear, Obedience and Salvation,
Volume 36, Sermon #2147 - Hebrews 11:7

A temporary hope is ill purchased at the cost of cruel disappointment.

The Peace of the Devil and the Peace of God,
Volume 36, Sermon #2157 - Luke 11:21, Psalm 29:11

You will never be on a right foundation until you are off the wrong one.

The Peace of the Devil and the Peace of God,
Volume 36, Sermon #2157 - Luke 11:21, Psalm 29:11

When the devil is not troubled by us, he does not trouble us.

Our Manifesto,
Volume 37, Sermon #2185 - Galatians 1:11

How very curiously people try to give God something else instead of what he asks for!

The Obedience of Faith,
Volume 37, Sermon #2195 - Hebrews 11:8

Do the right, even if the heavens should fall.

"My Times Are in Your Hand",
Volume 37, Sermon #2205 - Psalm 31:15

He that takes care of our times, will take care of our eternity.

"My Times Are in Your Hand",
Volume 37, Sermon #2205 - Psalm 31:15

A rock which is in nobody's way may stand where it is.

The Agreement of Salvation By Grace with Walking in Good Works,
Volume 37, Sermon #2210 - Ephesians 2:9, 10

Oh, for grace to love the rough paths, because we see his footprints upon them!

The Private Thoughts and Words of Jesus,
Volume 37, Sermon #2212 - Matthew 20:17-19

"Ignorance is the mother of devotion," according to the Church of Rome. "Ignorance is the mother of error," according to the Word of God.

Barriers Broken Down,
Volume 37, Sermon #2214 - Romans 10:3

Men's pennies and God's promises do not very well go together to buy heaven.

Barriers Broken Down,
Volume 37, Sermon #2214 - Romans 10:3

Only those who never do any spiritual work talk about what they can accomplish.

"Is the Spirit of the Lord Straitened?",
Volume 37, Sermon #2218 - Micah 2:7

By a life I do not live, and by a death I do not die, I am saved.

Abraham's Trial—A Lesson for Believers,
Volume 37, Sermon #2223 - Genesis 22:1

A long stretch of health has a tendency to make us think that we are immortal.

A Clarion Call to Saints and Sinners,
Volume 37, Sermon #2225 - Micah 2:10

It is strange that men should expect God to take their gift, when they refuse to accept his.

"Lay Hold On Eternal Life!",
Volume 37, Sermon #2226 - 1 Timothy 6:12

The Christian's position is unique: he is in two worlds at once.

"Lay Hold On Eternal Life!",
Volume 37, Sermon #2226 - 1 Timothy 6:12

He must die, or we must die, or justice must die.

God's Glorious and Everlasting Name,
Volume 37, Sermon #2229 - Isaiah 63:12, 14

Many a time our severity to others is the reason for God's apparent severity with us.

Both Sides of the Shield,
Volume 37, Sermon #2233 - Exodus 17:8, 9

He sees right through us at a glance, as if we were made of glass; he sees all our past, present, and future.

Prodigal Love for the Prodigal Son,
Volume 37, Sermon #2236 - Luke 15:20

The sacred Dove will never come to a foul nest.

"Is God in the Camp?",
Volume 38, Sermon #2239 - 1 Samuel 4:7

How can we reckon upon anything in a world like this, where nothing is certain but uncertainty?

God's Will About the Future,
Volume 38, Sermon #2242 - James 4:13-17

Put all your heart into what you do, or else put none of it in.

Words to Rest On,
Volume 38, Sermon #2250 - 2 Chronicles 32:8

Better to go to heaven as a hermit, than go to hell with a multitude.

The Two Guards Praying and Watching,
Volume 38, Sermon #2254 - Nehemiah 4:9

You will not attempt the work, and of course you will not complete what you do not commence.

Sowing in the Wind, Reaping Under Clouds,
Volume 38, Sermon #2264 - Ecclesiastes 11:4

What may happen from our doing right, we have nothing to do with; we are to do right, and take the consequences cheerfully.

Sowing in the Wind, Reaping Under Clouds,
Volume 38, Sermon #2264 - Ecclesiastes 11:4

The more you do for men, the less will be their return.

Alone, Yet Not Alone,
Volume 38, Sermon #2271 - John 16:31, 32

You shall read the evening of life in the morning of life, and you shall decide what your evening is to be by what your morning is.

"Dare to Be a Daniel",
Volume 39, Sermon #2291 - Daniel 1:8

There is nothing that the worst of men have done which the best of men could not do if they were left by the grace of God.

Saints Guarded from Stumbling,
Volume 39, Sermon #2296 - Jude 1:24, 25

Ah, yes, the power to do more oozes out by the leakage of contentment with what you have done!

Three Arrows—Or Six?,
Volume 39, Sermon #2303 - 2 Kings 13:18, 19

You were not saved that you might go to heaven alone; you were saved that you might take others there with you.

Twelve Covenant Mercies,
Volume 39, Sermon #2316 - Isaiah 55:3

Not a deed is done that dies, especially the deeds of quickened men and women.

Twelve Covenant Mercies,
Volume 39, Sermon #2316 - Isaiah 55:3

Where Scripture is silent, be you silent.

Obeying Christ's Orders,
Volume 39, Sermon #2317 - John 2:5

With many a mistake, with many a weakness, yet, beloved, the saints are free from falsehood.

The Followers of the Lamb,
Volume 39, Sermon #2324 - Revelation 14:4, 5

God thinks of every separate child of His as much as if He had only that one.

Lessons from the Manna,
Volume 39, Sermon #2332 - Exodus 16:4

Growing saints think themselves nothing; full-grown saints think themselves less than nothing.

Three Texts, But One Subject—Faith,
Volume 39, Sermon #2335 - Psalm 57:1, Psalm 55:22, Isaiah 51:10

Man must have a god; he cannot be happy without one.

Eternal Life!,
Volume 41, Sermon #2396 - John 17:3, 1 John 5:20, 21

In truth, there is nothing due from God to you but that he should let you perish in your sin; that is all he owes you.

Under Arrest,
Volume 41, Sermon #2402 - Galatians 3:23

I believe that the short way to the conversion of sinners is the sanctification of saints.

A Special Benediction,
Volume 41, Sermon #2412 - Jude 1, 2

The sternest predestination is not the least in conflict with the most perfect freedom of the human will.

A Cure for A Weak Heart,
Volume 42, Sermon #2455 - Psalm 31:24

I have heard of one who called life, "the long disease of life"; and it was so to him, for, though he did a great work for his Master, he was always sickly.

Job's Resignation,
Volume 42, Sermon #2457 - Job 1:20-22

And depend upon it, brothers, there is no way of bringing afflictions upon ourselves like refusing to bear afflictions.

"This Thing Is From Me",
Volume 42, Sermon #2476 - 1 Kings 12:24

This is the quintessence of delight that, when the saint gets to heaven, he will be as rightly there as the sinner in hell will be rightly there.

Singing Saints,
Volume 42, Sermon #2489 - Psalm 30:4

Christ loved you when he died; he will love you when you die.

Paul's Persuasion,
Volume 42, Sermon #2492 - Romans 8:38, 39

People don't lose diseases, generally, where they catch them.

A Lost Christ Found,
Volume 45, Sermon #2611 - Luke 2:44-46

In a free country like this, you may be almost anything you like except a Christian.

A Lost Christ Found,
Volume 45, Sermon #2611 - Luke 2:44-46

A man who makes a profession of religion ought to be something more than other people.

God's Work in Man,
Volume 45, Sermon #2629 - Hosea 2:16

The end of the creature is the beginning of the Creator. Your extremity is God's opportunity.

Israel's Cry and God's Answer,
Volume 45, Sermon #2631 - Exodus 2:23-25; 3:9, 10

There are none so brokenhearted as those that are brokenhearted because they are not brokenhearted.

Israel's Cry and God's Answer,
Volume 45, Sermon #2631 - Exodus 2:23-25; 3:9, 10

When a man blesses God for the bitter, the Lord often sends him the sweet. If he can praise God in the night, the daylight is not far off.

Comforted and Comforting,
Volume 45, Sermon #2640 - 2 Corinthians 1:3, 4

I confess that I would hardly give a penny for any salvation that I could lose; I would not go across the street to pick up a sort of quarterly or yearly salvation.

God's Heart the Source of All Blessing,
Volume 45, Sermon #2641 - 2 Samuel 7:21

Heathenism is hopeless to afford any comfort to the bereaved.

Fallen Asleep,
Volume 46, Sermon #2659 - 1 Corinthians 15:6

I intend to grasp tightly with one hand the truths I have already learned, and to keep the other hand wide open to take in the things I do not yet know.

Things Unknown,
Volume 46, Sermon #2664 - Jeremiah 33:3

If any man is content with his own experience, it is entirely through ignorance.

Things Unknown,
Volume 46, Sermon #2664 - Jeremiah 33:3

No man is so happy but he would be happier still if he had true religion.

Meditation on God,
Volume 46, Sermon #2690 - Psalm 104:34

Gift is but an addition to our load, but grace is strength with which to carry it.

Grace Preferred to Gifts,
Volume 46, Sermon #2694 - 1 Corinthians 12:31

The principle that rules us is not "Must I?" but "May I?" It becomes to the believer a joy and a delight to serve Christ; he is not flogged to his duty.

Jesus Joyfully Received,
Volume 46, Sermon #2701 - Luke 19:6

There is more to marvel at in half an inch of the way to heaven than there is in a thousand leagues of the ordinary pathway of unbelieving men.

"Marvelous Loving Kindness",
Volume 46, Sermon #2702 - Psalm 17:7

The Christian man, who trusts that, by any one sin, he may keep himself out of difficulty, or get himself out of difficulty, makes a terrible mistake.

The Preservation of Christians in the World,
Volume 46, Sermon #2703 - John 17:15

God never intends that there shall be any sweet in this world without something sour to go with it.

Bitter Herbs,
Volume 47, Sermon #2727 - Exodus 12:8

I know this; when my soul is full of Christ, I can defy the devil himself, for what can he bring me when I want nothing?

The Soul's Best Food,
Volume 48, Sermon #2786 - Isaiah 55:2

If you have lived to bring one sinner to Christ, you have not lived in vain.

A High Day in Heaven,
Volume 48, Sermon #2791 - Luke 15:10

There is nothing we have here below which is not somewhat tainted with grief.

A Refreshing Canticle,
Volume 48, Sermon #2794 - Solomon's Song 1:4

I do not expect fully to understand my Lord's will, I only ask to be informed what that will is.

"Nevertheless At Your Word",
Volume 48, Sermon #2810 - Luke 5:5

Sin and sorrow cannot be divorced, and holiness and happiness cannot be separated.

Life, and the Path to It,
Volume 49, Sermon #2813 - Psalm 16:11

The world was wisely ordered by God before we were born, and it will be equally well ordered by him after we are dead.

Conceit Rebuked,
Volume 49, Sermon #2834 - Job 34:33

Surely, a God whom we could understand would be no God.

God's Glory in Hiding Sin,
Volume 49, Sermon #2838 - Proverbs 25:2

The will of man is the source of damnation, and the will of God is the source of salvation.

Laying the Hand On the Sacrifice,
Volume 49, Sermon #2840 - Leviticus 4:29

Beware of having so much to do that you really do nothing at all because you do not wait upon God for the power to do it aright.

Lacking Moisture,
Volume 49, Sermon #2845 - Luke 8:6

God will not let us, who are his song-birds, build our nests here.

Our Hiding Place,
Volume 49, Sermon #2856 - Isaiah 32:2

Should everything seem to go amiss with us after we have done the right thing, there is no cause for regret. Remember that our conduct is the maker of our character.

The Lion's Den,
Volume 49, Sermon #2859 - Daniel 6:20

How you loathe a friend who will not stick to you in dark times!

The Lion's Den,
Volume 49, Sermon #2859 - Daniel 6:20

Divine wisdom arranges our lot, but our lots are not precisely alike.

Owl Or Eagle?,
Volume 49, Sermon #2860 - Psalm 102:6, Psalm 103:5

Better slay a single enemy than dream of slaughtering an army.

"The Time Is Short",
Volume 49, Sermon #2861 - 1 Corinthians 7:29

A grain of grace is worth more than a ton of knowledge.

The Way of Wisdom,
Volume 49, Sermon #2862 - Job 28:7, 8

If the Lord had ever meant us to fall into hell, we should have gone there years ago.

New Tokens of Ancient Love,
Volume 50, Sermon #2880 - Jeremiah 31:3

He who is his own guide is guided by a fool.

An Instructive Truth,
Volume 50, Sermon #2893 - Jeremiah 10:23

He intended to save men, but he never intended to gratify their depraved tastes.

A Mournful Defection,
Volume 50, Sermon #2914 - John 6:67

When a man is in trouble, help him out first, and then blame him for having got into it, if you feel it necessary to do so.

Reasons for Doubting Christ,
Volume 51, Sermon #2925 - Matthew 14:31

Stagnation is inconsistent with life.

Resistance to Salvation,
Volume 51, Sermon #2966 - Mark 5:7

But happy is the fish that fears the bait as well as the hook, and so keeps right away from both of them.

The Right Kind of Fear,
Volume 52, Sermon #2971 - Proverbs 28:14

Sufferings are only scars, flesh wounds; sins are the real woundings.

A Wafer of Honey,
Volume 52, Sermon #2974 - 2 Corinthians 12:9

The man, whose arm is not long enough to grasp that which lies in the land beyond the stars, will have to live and die without attaining to perfect satisfaction.

Plowing Rock,
Volume 52, Sermon #2977 - Amos 6:12

The only difference between a very wise man and a very great fool is that the wise man knows that he is a fool, and the other does not.

Come and Welcome,
Volume 52, Sermon #3000 - John 6:37

If we are careful about our little actions, the great ones will be pretty sure to be right.

The Best Thing in the Best Place,
Volume 52, Sermon #3002 - Psalm 37:31

If I may use such an expression, time is not the time for the manifestation of a Christian's glory.

The Christian's Manifestation,
Volume 52, Sermon #3004 - 1 John 3:2

You are not forgiven if you cannot forgive.

Good Cheer from Forgiven Sin,
Volume 52, Sermon #3016 - Matthew 9:2, Mark 2:3-5, Luke 5:18-20

We heard of a philosopher, who looked up to the stars, and fell into a pit; but, if they fall deeply who look up, how deeply do they fall who look down!

Vanity Deprecated,
Volume 53, Sermon #3026 - Psalm 119:37

If you are afraid of missing the spot you want to find, there is seldom anything lost by asking, and it is always better to spend one minute in asking the way than to waste ten minutes in going wrong.

Enquiring the Way to Zion,
Volume 53, Sermon #3035 - Jeremiah 50:5

It is better to go weeping to heaven than to go laughing to hell.

Enquiring the Way to Zion,
Volume 53, Sermon #3035 - Jeremiah 50:5

Each of God's saints is sent into the world to prove some part of the divine character.

Proving God,
Volume 53, Sermon #3036 - Malachi 3:10

Never mind where you work; care more about how you work!

Christ's Loneliness and Ours,
Volume 53, Sermon #3052 - John 16:31, 32

There are many things we wish for that we do not really need, but there is no promise given that we shall have all we wish for.

the Good Shepherd,
Volume 53, Sermon #3060 - Psalm 23:1

As long as you are forgiven, what does anything else matter?

A Bold Challenge Justified,
Volume 53, Sermon #3067 - Romans 8:34

The way of sense is to get everything now; the way of faith is to get everything in God's time.

An Observation of the Preacher,
Volume 53, Sermon #3072 - Ecclesiastes 7:8

Every wreck ought to be a beacon. One man's fall should be another man's warning.

Danger. Safety. Gratitude,
Volume 54, Sermon #3074 - Jude 1:24, 25

The man who knows something, and yet trifles with it, is not likely to be further instructed of God.

A Question for You,
Volume 55, Sermon #3132 - John 9:35

Be on God's side, I pray you, for that is the winning side.

Established Work,
Volume 55, Sermon #3142 - Psalm 90:17

I would sooner be despised with the orthodox than reign with "the intellectual."

Paul in the Tempest,
Volume 55, Sermon #3145 - Acts 27:18-25

Men go astray from God by nature, but they only return to God through grace.

Christ's Ambassadors,
Volume 55, Sermon #3148 - 2 Corinthians 5:20

Everyone who rules over men, though it be but over a petty nation or a small parish, knows that, if the law has no penalties attached to it, it ceases to have any power.

Christ's Ambassadors,
Volume 55, Sermon #3148 - 2 Corinthians 5:20

God gives you faith, but you must believe. God gives you repentance, but you must repent.

The Commissariat of the Universe,
Volume 55, Sermon #3149 - Psalm 104:28

The first object of the Christian is to glorify God, and the next object is to make other people happy.

The Lower Courts,
Volume 55, Sermon #3152 - 1 John 3:20, 21

The most of men do not think.

"A Greater Than Solomon",
Volume 55, Sermon #3166 - Matthew 12:42

Heaven and holiness are twin sisters.

The Believer's Present Rest,
Volume 55, Sermon #3169 - Hebrews 4:3

Happy are they who can follow a good cause in its worst estate, for theirs is true glory.

The Man Whose Hand Stuck to His Sword,
Volume 56, Sermon #3193 - 2 Samuel 23:9, 10

Surely, it needs little faith to believe in providence when the purse is full.

Faith Hand in Hand with Fear,
Volume 57, Sermon #3253 - Psalm 56:3

He that takes his brother by the throat will be sure to be taken by the throat himself.

Thoughts and Their Fruit,
Volume 57, Sermon #3257 - Jeremiah 6:19

God would have us all educated for the skies.

Intelligent Obedience,
Volume 57, Sermon #3263

Foolish loves make rods for foolish backs.

How to Become Full of Joy,
Volume 57, Sermon #3272 - 1 John 1:4

And men are indeed fools when they prefer the shadows of time to the substance of eternity.

Sickness and Prayer, Healing and Praise,
Volume 57, Sermon #3274 - Psalm 107:17-22

He preaches pardon to those who know that they have sinned, and confess the same; but those who have no sin have no Savior.

Christ the Seeker and Savior of the Lost,
Volume 58, Sermon #3309 - Luke 19:10

"The Holy Spirit helps us in our infirmities," but not our idlenesses.

How to Read the Bible,
Volume 58, Sermon #3318 - 1 Timothy 4:13

This seems to be a world of trying rather than of accomplishing.

The Believer's Glad Prospects,
Volume 58, Sermon #3323 - Solomon's Song 2:17

You need not be so much afraid of that which grieves you as of that which charms you.

Things to Be Remembered,
Volume 59, Sermon #3347 - Psalm 38:(Title)

The external is generally painted from within.

"The Garment of Praise",
Volume 59, Sermon #3349 - Isaiah 61:3

We are never so weak as when we think we are strong, and never so strong as when we know we are weak, and look out of ourselves to our God.

Two Choice Benedictions,
Volume 59, Sermon #3371 - Numbers 6:23-27, 2 Corinthians 13:14

Every true child of God would sooner sorrow a thousand times than sin once.

Standing and Singing,
Volume 59, Sermon #3375 - Psalm 26:12

And if he emptied his great self for us, who are as nothing, shall not we be ready to empty our little selves for him, who is so great?

Our Lord's Voluntary Poverty,
Volume 59, Sermon #3380 - 2 Corinthians 8:9

Eminent usefulness usually necessitates eminent affliction.

Soul-Threshing,
Volume 60, Sermon #3388 - Isaiah 28:27, 28

No man can put on the robes of Christ's righteousness till he has taken off his own.

Sharing Christ's Life,
Volume 60, Sermon #3401 - John 14:19

Never do what you are ashamed of; it matters not who sees.

Buying the Truth,
Volume 61, Sermon #3449 - Proverbs 23:23

It cannot be that God has left the world; it must be that the world has left God.

A Message from God,
Volume 61, Sermon #3455 - Judges 3:20

Heed not the world's frowns, and court not its smiles.

All Are Guilty,
Volume 61, Sermon #3457 - Matthew 27:22, 23

Devils could not be worse than men when their passions are let loose.

A New Creation,
Volume 61, Sermon #3467 - Revelation 21:5

Precept has no regenerative power. People do not get good by having goodness preached at them.

Araunah's Threshing Floor,
Volume 61, Sermon #3477 - 1 Chronicles 22:1

Unbelief will destroy the best of us: faith will save the worst of us.

The Judgement Upon Zacharias,
Volume 62, Sermon #3495 - Luke 1:20

It is not always that the thing which makes us glad to-day will make us glad to-morrow likewise.

A Miracle of Grace,
Volume 62, Sermon #3505 - 2 Chronicles 33:9-13

Where God works, he works with men that work.

The Powerful Truth of God,
Volume 62, Sermon #3518 - Acts 19:19, 20

What sin is worth being damned for?

An Earnest Entreaty,
Volume 63, Sermon #3550 - Psalm 2:12

Self-Righteousness

There is no attribute of God which self-righteousness does not impugn.

Words of Advice, Page 6

Self-righteousness arises partly from pride, but mainly from ignorance of God's law.

Secret Sins,
Volume 3, Sermon #116 - Psalm 19:12

How much does a man love himself? None of us too little, some of us too much.

Love Your Neighbor,
Volume 3, Sermon #145 - Matthew 19:19

Ever since man became a sinner he has been self-righteous. When he had a righteousness of his own he never gloried of it, but ever since he has lost it, he has pretended to be the possessor of it.

A Blow at Self-Righteousness,
Volume 7, Sermon #350 - Job 9:20

When you feel yourself to be utterly unworthy, you have hit the truth.

Unsound Spiritual Trading,
Volume 15, Sermon #849 - Proverbs 16:2

The fact that Christ died for the ungodly renders self-righteousness a folly.

For Whom Did Christ Die?,
Volume 20, Sermon #1191 - Romans 5:6

Would God have taken the trouble to make another righteousness if you could have made one of your own?

Zealous, But Wrong,
Volume 32, Sermon #1899 - Romans 10:1, 2, 3

The saint most ripe for heaven is the most aware of his own shortcomings.

Two Essential Things,
Volume 35, Sermon #2073 - Acts 20:21

Some of the Lord's workers have grown so big that the least thing offends them; everything must be according to their own way, or they will have nothing to do with it.

A Hard Case,
Volume 42, Sermon #2453 - Job 33:14-18

It is easy for the Lord to save a sinner, but it is impossible for a self-righteous man to be saved until he is brought down from his fatal pride.

A Hard Case,
Volume 42, Sermon #2453 - Job 33:14-18

He who is his own guide is guided by a fool. He that trusts to his own understanding proves that he has no understanding.

An Instructive Truth,
Volume 50, Sermon #2893 - Jeremiah 10:23

Self-satisfaction is the death of progress. Contentment with worldly goods is a blessing, but contentment in spiritual things is a curse and a sin.

The Hungry Filled, the Rich Emptied,
Volume 52, Sermon #3019 - Luke 1:53

Self-esteem naturally keeps Jesus out of the heart. And the more our self- esteem increases, the more firmly do we fasten the door against Christ. Love of self prevents love of the Savior!

Why Christ Is Not Esteemed,
Volume 53, Sermon #3033 - Isaiah 53:3

Self and the Savior can never live in one heart. He will have all, or none. So, where self is on the throne, it cannot be expected that Christ should meekly come and sit upon the footstool.

Why Christ Is Not Esteemed,
Volume 53, Sermon #3033 - Isaiah 53:3

The greatest enemy to human souls—I think I am not wrong in saying this—is the self-righteous spirit which makes men look to themselves for salvation.

Soul Satisfaction,
Volume 55, Sermon #3137 - Psalm 35:3

If you are not spared, but perish, it will not be because God is not merciful to you but because you are not merciful to yourselves!

Turning from Death,
Volume 58, Sermon #3324 - Ezekiel 33:11

Holy anxiety to be found sincere and acceptable with God prevents all self-confidence.

Solace for Sad Hearts,
Volume 58, Sermon #3325 - Isaiah 61:3

He is the physician for any form of disease, except that form of disease which consists in not being diseased.

Man Humbled, God Exalted,
Volume 59, Sermon #3369 - Isaiah 2:17

Sermons

One of these days you will want a microscope to find a grain of evangelical doctrine in a dozen sermons.

Profitable Mixture,
Volume 35, Sermon #2089 - Hebrews 4:2

In fact, there is no worship of God that is better than the hearing of a sermon.

The Blessings of Public Worship,
Volume 41, Sermon #2395 - Luke 18:10

Sin

The sins of to-day are the sorrows of ages.

An All Around Ministry, Page 234

Men by their sins have forfeited all claim upon God; they deserve to perish for their sins—and if they all do so, they have no ground for complaint.

Morning and Evening, Page 661

God's people can never by any possibility be punished for their sins.

Words of Cheer, Page 66

Be sure your sin will find you out, and it will generally find you out here.

Words of Wisdom, Page 43

It is easy to commit sin, but hard to confess it. Man will transgress without a tempter; but even when urged by the most earnest pleader, he will not acknowledge his guilt.

A Sight of Self,
Volume 8, Sermon #437 - Isaiah 64:6, 7, 8

Chosen vessels of mercy, notwithstanding their backslidings, are brought back; but ah! remember that nine out of ten of those who backslide never were God's people.

The Backslider's Way Hedged Up,
Volume 10, Sermon #590 - Hosea 2:5-7

You must plead "Guilty," or remain guilty for ever.

Confession of Sin
Illustrated By the Cases of Dr. Pritchard and Constance Kent,
Volume 11, Sermon #641 - Psalm 32:5

As far as God is concerned your sin has ceased to be.

The Heart Full and the Mouth Closed,
Volume 22, Sermon #1289 - Ezekiel 16:62, 63

There is mercy for a sinner, but there is no mercy for the man who will not own himself a sinner.

Peace—A Fact and a Feeling,
Volume 25, Sermon #1456 - Romans 5:1

A few minutes' folly may ruin years of character.

My Hourly Prayer,
Volume 28, Sermon #1657 - Psalm 119:117

Sin virtually committed suicide when it slew the Savior, for his death became its death.

Shutting, Sealing and Covering,
Volume 28, Sermon #1681 - Daniel 9:24

Sin reached its finis, its ultimatum, its climax, in the murder of the Son of God.

Shutting, Sealing and Covering,
Volume 28, Sermon #1681 - Daniel 9:24

All sorts of sins may hide away in one sin.

The Annual Atonement,
Volume 32, Sermon #1923 - Leviticus 16:30

A sinner is like a man possessed with a devil who cries, "My name is Legion: for we are many."

The Annual Atonement,
Volume 32, Sermon #1923 - Leviticus 16:30

Sin has been pardoned at such a price that we cannot henceforth trifle with it.

The Annual Atonement,
Volume 32, Sermon #1923 - Leviticus 16:30

The sting of affliction lies in the tail of our rebellion against the divine will.

The Lover of God's Law Filled with Peace,
Volume 34, Sermon #2004 - Psalm 119:165

The more God loves you, and the more you love God, the more expensive will you find it to sin. An ordinary sinner sins cheaply: the child of God sins very dearly.

Peter After His Restoration,
Volume 34, Sermon #2035 - Luke 22:32

If you believe, [in God], your belief will kill your sinning, or else your sinning will kill your believing! The greatest argument against the Bible is an unholy life—and when a man will give that up, he will convince himself.

No Fixity Without Faith,
Volume 39, Sermon #2305 - Isaiah 7:9

There would be nobody to receive mercy if nobody were guilty.

A Page From A Royal Diary,
Volume 40, Sermon #2372 - Psalm 119:132

When a man sins outwardly, it is because he has sin inwardly. If there were no sin in us, no sin would come out of us.

A Singular Plea in Prayer,
Volume 43, Sermon #2535 - Psalm 41:4

There are two kinds of tears and I think that they who truly seek the Lord shed both of them—the one is a tear of sorrow because of sin, the other is a tear of joy because of pardon.

A Test for True Seekers,
Volume 44, Sermon #2566 - Jeremiah 50:5

Nowhere in the whole compass of Revelation is there a promise of forgiveness to the man who continues his iniquity!

The Need and Nature of Conversion,
Volume 48, Sermon #2797 - Isaiah 55:7

There are no men who are in such danger as the men who think they are not in any danger! There are none so likely to sin as those who say they cannot sin!

Startling!,
Volume 49, Sermon #2828 - 2 Kings 8:12, 13

It is the devil who renders evil for good, yet you are sinking to his level if you continue in sin and turn not unto God who has dealt so kindly and so graciously with you.

God's Goodness Leading to Repentance,
Volume 49, Sermon #2857 - Romans 2:4

How can we remember his death without sorrowing over the sin which made that death necessary?

Christ's Crowning Glory,
Volume 50, Sermon #2876 - Psalm 21:5

Nine times out of ten, declension from God begins in the neglect of private prayer.

Return! Return!,
Volume 51, Sermon #2931 - Jeremiah 3:12, 14, 22

As the volcano is but the index of a mighty seething ocean of devouring flame within the heart of the earth, so any one sin is only a token of far greater sinfulness that seethes and boils within the cauldron of our nature! "Behold, I was shapen in iniquity; and in sin did my mother conceive me."

Our Champion,
Volume 52, Sermon #3009 - Judges 16:3

It is an unspeakable blessing to have sin forgiven.

Christians Kept from Sin,
Volume 53, Sermon #3037 - 1 Samuel 25:32, 33

Sin is an everlasting thing—unless it is put away by God, Himself, for the Lord Jesus Christ's sake—no grave in the world can hide it.

Filling Up the Measure of Iniquity,
Volume 53, Sermon #3043 - Genesis 15:16

Man, you must die in your sins if you continue to live in them! You cannot escape from the consequence of sin if you keep following in the pursuit of sin. Work and you shall have your wages—and "the wages of sin is death."

Filling Up the Measure of Iniquity,
Volume 53, Sermon #3043 - Genesis 15:16

Light thoughts of sin breed light thoughts of the Savior.

"Going and Weeping",
Volume 53, Sermon #3049 - Jeremiah 50:4

Be ever afraid of not being afraid, and be always in fear when you feel that you are perfectly safe.

Danger. Safety. Gratitude.,
Volume 54, Sermon #3074 - Jude 1:24, 25

If you are not guilty, the Savior will not save you! If you are not a sinner, you have no part in Christ. If you can say, "I have kept the Law from my youth up and am not a transgressor," then we have no Gospel blessings to set before you.

A Sermon on a Grand Old Text,
Volume 54, Sermon #3089 - 1 Timothy 1:15

The power that is to fight and overcome sin is never described in the Word of God as the natural goodness of human nature.

Sin and Grace,
Volume 54, Sermon #3115 - Romans 5:20

Christ never came to be the minister of sin. He came to save us, not in our sins, but from our sins.

The Water and the Blood,
Volume 58, Sermon #3311 - John 19:34

Living in sin is the germ of living for ever in perdition.

Resurrection for the Just and the Unjust,
Volume 59, Sermon #3346 - Acts 24:15

To contend against Omnipotence is insanity.

An Earnest Entreaty,
Volume 63, Sermon #3550 - Psalm 2:12

Sovereignty

We are too insignificant to be of any great importance in God's vast universe; He can do either with us or without us, and our presence or absence will not disarrange His plans.

An All Around Ministry, Page 62

If the disposal of the lot is the Lord's, whose is the arrangement of our whole life?

Morning and Evening, Page 708

Our life is made up of trifles, and if we had a God only for the great things, and not for the little things, we should be miserable indeed.

Words of Wisdom, Page 95

When God appoints, none alter it.

Constancy and Inconstancy—A Contrast,
Volume 15, Sermon #852

He has fixed the hour of our entrance into rest, and it can neither be postponed by skill of physician nor hastened by malice of foe.

Crossing the Jordan,
Volume 34, Sermon #2039 - Joshua 1:10, 11

If the Lord has done it, questions are out of the question; and truly the Lord has done it. There may be a secondary agent, there probably is; the devil himself may be that secondary agent, yet the Lord has done it.

"The King Can Do No Wrong",
Volume 41, Sermon #2420 - 2 Samuel 3:36

We talk of "Providences" when we have hairbreadth escapes—but are they not quite as much Providences when we are preserved from danger?

God's Innumerable Mercies,
Volume 53, Sermon #3022 - Psalm 71:15

Opposition to divine sovereignty is essentially atheism. Men have no objection to a god who is really no God; I mean, by this, a god who shall be the subject of their caprice, who shall be a lackey to their will, who shall be under their control,—they have no objection to such a being as that; but a God who speaks, and it is done, who commands, and it stands fast, a God who has no respect for their persons, but does as he wills among the armies of heaven and among the inhabitants of this lower world, such a God as this they cannot endure.

"It Pleased God",
Volume 56, Sermon #3202 - Galatians 1:15

If you could have chosen your own circumstances and condition in life, you could not have made so wise a choice as God has made for you.

The Gospel Cordial,
Volume 57, Sermon #3236 - Proverbs 31:6, 7

No Doctrine in the whole Word of God has more excited the hatred of mankind than the truth of the absolute Sovereignty of God.

The Sequel to Divine Sovereignty,
Volume 58, Sermon #3284 - Psalm 97:1, 99:1

Spiritual Discipline

A smile from Jesus in the morning will be sunshine all the day.

Barbed Arrows, Page 15

The morning hour carries gold in its mouth.

John Ploughman's Talk, Page 143

He who does not long to know more of Christ, knows nothing of Him yet.

Morning and Evening, Page 8

Thus there will be three effects of nearness to Jesus—humility, happiness, and holiness.

Morning and Evening, Page 266

He who communes with God is always at home.

The Treasury of David, Psalm 61, Verse 4

Sin is usually at the bottom of all the hidings of the Lord's face; let us ask the Lord to reveal the special form of it to us, that we may repent of it, overcome it, and henceforth forsake it.

The Treasury of David, Psalm 74, Verse 1

Communion is the mother of adoration.

The Treasury of David, Psalm 84, Verse 4

We want one of the two—either to commune with God, or else to sigh and cry till we do so.

Concerning Prayer,
Volume 34, Sermon #2053 - Psalm 86:6, 7

A sitting silently at the feet of Jesus is of more worth than all the clatter of Martha's dishes.

Breakfast with Jesus,
Volume 35, Sermon #2072 - John 21:12

A child of God should not leave his bedroom in the morning without being on good terms with his God.

A Delicious Experience,
Volume 35, Sermon #2090 - Hebrews 4:3

Sinning will make you leave off communion with God, or else communion with God will make you leave off sinning: one of the two things must occur.

The Warnings and the Rewards of the Word of God,
Volume 36, Sermon #2135 - Psalm 19:11

The active life will have little power in it if it is not accompanied by much of the contemplative and the prayerful.

Christ's Transfigured Face,
Volume 47, Sermon #2729 - Matthew 17:2

I believe that we make more real advance in the divine life in an hour of prayer than we do in a month of sermon-hearing.

The Beauty of the Olive Tree,
Volume 55, Sermon #3176 - Hosea 14:6

You have but one day in the week, as it were, devoted to these things; one day of building, and six of pulling down. With many it is one day's storing, and six days scattering. It is but a slight advance that we make towards heaven.

The Great Teacher and Remembrancer,
Volume 59, Sermon #3353 - John 14:26

Brethren, let us never sit down content with small degrees of sanctification.

A Definite Challenge for Definite Prayer,
Volume 62, Sermon #3537 - Mark 10:51

Substitution

We believe in the real, literal substitution of Christ in the place of all whom He had covenanted to save, and as many as believe in Him may know assuredly that their sins were transferred from them and laid upon Him!

The Soul's Food and Drink,
Volume 56, Sermon #3192 - John 6:55

Success

My brethren, we are not half-Christians; that is the reason why we have not half-success.

Gospel Missions,
Volume 2, Sermon #76 - Acts 13:49

Great success is like a full cup, it is hard to hold it with a steady hand. It is swimming in deep waters, and there is always a fear of being drowned there. It is standing on the top of the pinnacle of the temple, and Satan often says, "Cast thyself down."

Humility,
Volume 7, Sermon #365 - Acts 20:19

Lend me a spiritual thermometer by which I may try the heat of your heart, and I will tell you the amount of your success.

Life in Earnest,
Volume 8, Sermon #433 - 2 Chronicles 31:21

I think we are no judges of how we do our work—that the Master knows better than we do the success of our enterprises. Beside, dear friends, you do not expect to see fruit at once, do you? "Cast thy bread upon the waters, and thou shalt find it after many days." You have not had the "many days" to wait yet.

Songs for Desolate Hearts,
Volume 11, Sermon #649 - Isaiah 54:1

No man ever succeeds in anything who does not give himself wholly to it: it matters not what it is, concentration is essential to perfection in any pursuit. He who would be eminent in any one direction must forego a great many other things which are perfectly allowable; these he must renounce for the sake of his one object. He will not succeed unless he sacrifices all other things to the one chief thing.

"Without Carefulness",
Volume 28, Sermon #1692 - 1 Corinthians 7:32

Sunday School

You Sunday school teachers will always teach well when you go down to the schoolroom through the Door, that is, having been with Christ, having sought and enjoyed His company.

The Only Door,
Volume 58, Sermon #3287 - John 10:9

Tears

Tears are the diamonds of heaven; sighs are a part of the music of Jehovah's court, and are numbered with "the sublimest strains that reach the majesty on high."

Morning and Evening, Page 616

Is it not sweet to believe that our tears are understood even when words fail! Let us learn to think of tears as liquid prayers, and of weeping as a constant dropping of importunate intercession which will wear its way right surely into the very heart of mercy, despite the stony difficulties which obstruct the way.

The Treasury of David, Psalm 6, Verse 8

A tear is enough water to float a desire to God.

An Assuredly Good Thing,
Volume 15, Sermon #879 - Psalm 73:28

Why are we troubled? Is there anything worth shedding a tear for now that all is well for eternity?

The Jewel of Peace,
Volume 23, Sermon #1343 - 2 Thessalonians 3:16

When you are so weak that you cannot do much more than cry, you coin diamonds with both your eyes. The sweetest prayers God ever hears are the groans and sighs of those who have no hope in anything but his love.

The Cast-off Sash,
Volume 29, Sermon #1706 - Jeremiah 13:1-11

People die of bursting hearts when no tears relieve them.

Peter's Restoration,
Volume 34, Sermon #2034 - Luke 22:60-62

Turn the vessel upside down; it is a good thing to empty it, for this grief may ferment into something more sour. Turn the vessel upside down, and let every drop run out; but let it be before the Lord.

Job's Resignation,
Volume 42, Sermon #2457 - Job 1:20-22

When they begin to live to Christ they begin to mourn. Every child of God is born again with a tear in his eye. Dry-eyed faith is not the faith of God's elect. He who rejoices in Christ at the same time mourns for sin. Repentance is joined to faith by loving bands, as the Siamese twins were united in one.

Solace for Sad Hearts,
Volume 58, Sermon #3325 - Isaiah 61:3

Thought

Little things please little minds, and nasty things please dirty minds.

John Ploughman's Pictures, Page 81

We ought to mind our thoughts, for if they turn to be our enemies, they will be too many for us, and will drag us down to ruin.

John Ploughman's Talk, Page 61

We cannot help the birds flying over our heads; but we may keep them from building their nests in our hair.

John Ploughman's Talk, Page 63

Though sinful thoughts rise, they must not reign.

John Ploughman's Talk, Page 63

Good men are none the less full of thought because they are men of faith: believing is not the death of thinking, it is the sanctification of it.

Medicine for the Distracted,
Volume 19, Sermon #1116 - Psalm 94:19

If all the thoughts of the chastest and holiest here could now be unveiled to all, a life-enduring blush would crimson every cheek.

Medicine for the Distracted,
Volume 19, Sermon #1116 - Psalm 94:19

Thinking is a kind of work which the mass of the present race abhor.

Why Men Cannot Believe in Christ,
Volume 21, Sermon #1245 - John 5:44

Deep thinking is a very shallow affair after all when the thoughts are our own; we only get into real depths when we receive the thoughts of God.

God Glorified By Children's Mouths,
Volume 26, Sermon #1545 - Psalm 8:2

Thoughts are the eggs of words and actions, and within the thoughts lie compacted and condensed all the villainy of actual transgressions.

Hideous Discovery,
Volume 32, Sermon #1911 - Mark 7:20-23

If our thoughts run upon care and pleasure, they cannot be eager about true religion: is that not clear?

Sown Among Thorns,
Volume 34, Sermon #2040 - Matthew 13:7, 22

It is certain that thoughts are the eggs of sin.

Thoughts and Their Fruit,
Volume 57, Sermon #3257 - Jeremiah 6:19

Trials

Every sufferer who bears pain, or slander, or loss, or personal unkindness for Christ's sake, is filling up that amount of suffering which is necessary to the bringing together of the whole body of Christ, and the upbuilding of His elect Church.

An All Around Ministry, Page 383

I venture to say that the greatest earthly blessing that God can give to any of us is health, with the exception of sickness. Sickness has frequently been of more use to the saints of God than health has.

An All Around Ministry, Page 384

Our lusts are cords. Fiery trials are sent to burn and consume them. Who fears the flame which will bring him liberty from bonds intolerable?

Feathers for Arrows, Page 138

Pain past is pleasure, and experience comes by it.

John Ploughman's Talk, Page 41

The best remedy for affliction is submitting to providence. What can't be cured must be endured.

John Ploughman's Talk, Page 44

How happy are tried Christians, afterwards.

Morning and Evening, Page 279

Better suffer from childhood to old age than to be let alone to find pleasure in sin.

The Treasury of David, Psalm 88, Verse 15

Great hearts can only be made by great troubles.

Words of Cheer, Page 24

God always chastises his children twice if they do not bear the first blow patiently.

Words of Cheer, Page 69

Our sorrows shall have an end when God has gotten his end in them.

Intercessory Prayer, Volume 7, Sermon #404 - Job 42:10

My brethren, if God sent us trials such as we would wish for, they would be no trials.

Chastisement-Now and Afterwards,
Volume 9, Sermon #528 - Hebrews 12:11

God's rod flogs his child not from him, but to him.

For the Troubled,
Volume 19, Sermon #1090 - Psalm 88:7

Mighty prayer has often been produced by mighty trial.

With the Disciples on the Lake of Galilee, V
olume 28, Sermon #1686 - Matthew 8:27, Mark 4:41

Victory needs conflict as its preface.

Gladness for Sadness,
Volume 29, Sermon #1701 - Psalm 90:15-17

If there are no adversaries, you may fear that there will be no success.

Two Pauls and a Blinded Sorcerer,
Volume 30, Sermon #1781 - Acts 13:12

Untried faith is questionable faith. Is it faith at all?

A Discourse Upon True Blessedness Here and Hereafter,
Volume 31, Sermon #1874 - James 1:12

You pray against promotion when you pray against affliction.

Love at Its Utmost,
Volume 33, Sermon #1982 - John 15:9

We never have yet experienced a trouble which might not have been worse.

Gratitude for Deliverance from the Grave,
Volume 38, Sermon #2237 - Psalm 118:17, 18

In any labour to which we set our hand, if we take too much notice of the difficulties, we shall be hindered in it.

Sowing in the Wind, Reaping Under Clouds,
Volume 38, Sermon #2264 - Ecclesiastes 11:4

There is no University for a Christian like that of sorrow and trial.

Marah Better Than Elim,
Volume 39, Sermon #2301 - Exodus 15:22-26

In the greatness of our troubles there may often be space for the greater display of the goodness of God!

Christ the Cure for Troubled Hearts,
Volume 41, Sermon #2408 - Luke 24:38

God had one Son without sin, but not a single child without the rod.

The Education of Sons of God,
Volume 47, Sermon #2722 - Hebrews 5:8

If sicknesses do not soften, they harden.

Migratory Birds,
Volume 49, Sermon #2858 - Jeremiah 8:7

A way is none the less right because it is rough. Indeed, often it is all the more sure to be the right way because it is so displeasing to flesh and blood.

Angelic Protection in Appointed Ways,
Volume 52, Sermon #2969 - Psalm 91:11

Conflicts bring experience and experience brings that growth in Grace which is not to be attained by any other means!

A Wafer of Honey,
Volume 52, Sermon #2974 - 2 Corinthians 12:9

To be one of the Lord's saved ones is joy enough to bear up the heart under every affliction!

Good Cheer from Grace Received,
Volume 53, Sermon #3020 - Matthew 9:20-22, Luke 8:42-48

The groans of earth shall be surpassed by the songs of heaven, and the woes of time shall be swallowed up in the hallelujahs of eternity.

Maroth-Or, the Disappointed,
Volume 56, Sermon #3184 - Micah 1:12

The discerning of the hand of God [in our afflictions] is a sweet lesson in the school of experience.

Woe and Weal,
Volume 57, Sermon #3239 - Micah 7:9

You have not gone where Jesus has not gone! No, the way in which you have gone was first trodden by Him. In all your afflictions He was afflicted and, therefore we say to you, "Why do you doubt?" Your trial was peculiar to you, but not to Him!

Unreasonable Reasons,
Volume 57, Sermon #3247 - Matthew 14:31

The safest part of a Christian's life is the time of his trial...Smooth water on the way to Heaven is always a sign that the soul should keep wide awake, for danger is near!

Fathomless,
Volume 59, Sermon #3368 - Psalm 36:6

Anybody's dog will follow me if I feed it, but only my own dog will follow me if I beat it.

The Saint's Trials and the Divine Deliverances,
Volume 63, Sermon #3548 - Psalm 77:1-20

Temptations

God had one Son without sin; but He has no son without temptation.

Morning and Evening, Page 81

We must always be on our watch against Satan, because, like a thief, he gives no intimation of his approach.

Morning and Evening, Page 81

Your occupation may be as humble as log splitting, and yet the devil can tempt you in it.

Morning and Evening, Page 645

Beware of beginnings: he who does not take the first wrong step will not take the second.

John Ploughman's Pictures, Page 117

Satan never brushes the feathers of his birds the wrong way; he generally deals with us according to our tastes and likings. He flavors his bait to his fish.

Satanic Hindrances,
Volume 11, Sermon #657 - 1 Thessalonians 2:18

Character often hinges on a day's resolve.

The Inner Side of Conversion,
Volume 35, Sermon #2104 - Jeremiah 31:18-20

Take heed, my brother, when you are tempted; for the next minute may be the pivot of your life.

The Inner Side of Conversion,
Volume 35, Sermon #2104 - Jeremiah 31:18-20

Voluntary continuance on evil ground leads to repeated temptations.

"In the Garden with Him",
Volume 35, Sermon #2106 - John 18:26

Gratitude bars the door against sin. Great love received overthrows great temptation to wander.

Perseverance in Holiness,
Volume 35, Sermon #2108 - Jeremiah 32:40

Great gifts are not great Graces, but great gifts require great Graces to go with them, or else they become a temptation and a snare.

Partnership with Christ,
Volume 44, Sermon #2580 - 1 Corinthians 1:9

God had one Son without sin, but He never had a son without temptation. The natural man is born to trouble as the sparks fly upward—and the Christian is born to temptation just as certainly and necessarily.

"Tempted of the Devil",
Volume 52, Sermon #2997 - Matthew 4:1

"There is no devil," said one, "like having no devil." That is to say, there is no temptation like the temptation of not being tempted!

Warning and Encouragement,
Volume 52, Sermon #3013 - Song of Solomon 5:2

The temptations that trouble me I would rather endure than encounter any fresh ones.

The Wandering Bird,
Volume 61, Sermon #3453 - Proverbs 27:8

The Trinity

To believe and love the Trinity is to possess the key of theology.

"Bread Enough and to Spare",
Volume 17, Sermon #1000 - Luke 15:17

It needs the Trinity to new-create a soul. Oh, Triune God, our souls which are new created worship you with the trinity of their nature—spirit, soul, and body.

The First Day of Creation,
Volume 21, Sermon #1252 - Genesis 1:4

We can never understand how Father, Son, and Holy Spirit can be three and yet one. for my part, I have long ago given up any desire to understand this great mystery, for I am perfectly satisfied that, if I could understand it, it would not be true, because God, from the very nature of things, must be incomprehensible.

The Saints' Love to God,
Volume 51, Sermon #2958 - Psalm 31:23

No study in Scripture is more interesting or profitable to the Christian than the revelation which is given to us concerning the Sacred Trinity, and the various parts which the divine Persons take in the work of our salvation.

A Promise and Precedent,
Volume 55, Sermon #3127 - John 16:14

Thus, then, you have the Son suffering for you, the Spirit applying to you the merit of his atoning sacrifice, and the Father well pleased with you because you are trusting in his beloved Son. Or, to put the truth in another form, the Father gives the great gospel feast, the Son is the feast, and the Spirit not only brings the invitations, but he also gathers the guests around the table.

Lessons from Christ's Baptism,
Volume 58, Sermon #3298 - Matthew 3:16, 17

Truth

He is not righteous who is not always righteous.

A Good Start, Page 289

A quiet conscience is a little heaven.

Barbed Arrows, Page 15

Better in the abyss of truth than on the summit of falsehood.

Barbed Arrows, Page 22

The line of truth is narrow as a razor's edge.

Barbed Arrows, Page 280

The safest truth is the simplest.

Barbed Arrows, Page 281

Some men profess a great deal; but we must not believe any one unless we see that his deeds answer to what he says.

Morning and Evening, Page 266

If truth is optional, error is justifiable.

The Down Grade Controversy, Page 66

I question whether truth has not generally to be with the minority, and whether it is not quite as honorable to serve God with two or three as it would be with two or three millions.

Words of Wisdom, Page 111

Your conscience is not the rule of your duty, but God's Word is; and if God's Word commands it, whatever your conscience may say about it, you are sinning if you refuse to obey.

Tell It All,
Volume 9, Sermon #514 - Mark 5:33

Truth will only be desired by true men.

Suffering and Reigning with Jesus,
Volume 10, Sermon #547 - 2 Timothy 2:12

By the ever-living God there is truth somewhere, and that truth we will find out if we can; and, having found it, we will hold it fast.

Good Cause for Great Zeal,
Volume 19, Sermon #1097 - Ezra 4:14

Men of the world are apt to say, "You are such a set of bigots; you think everybody wrong but yourselves." Is it wonderful that if we think we are right, we do not believe that those who are opposed to us can be right also?

"I and the Children",
Volume 20, Sermon #1194 - Isaiah 8:18

Truth is never stronger than when it walks with charity.

Supposing Him to Have Been in the Company,
Volume 29, Sermon #1724 - Luke 2:44

We hope to understand the truth better, but we shall never discover better truth.

Fathers in Christ,
Volume 29, Sermon #1751 - 1 John 2:13, 14

He that perverts truth shall soon be incapable of knowing the true from the false. If you persist in wearing glasses that distort, everything will be distorted to you.

Israel and Britain-A Note of Warning,
Volume 31, Sermon #1844 - John 12:37-41

Christianity is a life which grows out of truth.

Our Lord's Prayer for His People's Sanctification,
Volume 32, Sermon #1890 - John 17:17

He who hates truth soon hates its advocate.

A Cheering Incident At Bethabara,
Volume 32, Sermon #1924 - John 10:39-42

Hard words, if they be true, are better than soft words, if they be false.

The Best Bread,
Volume 33, Sermon #1940 - John 6:48

Long ago I ceased to count heads. Truth is usually in the minority in this evil world.

"Behold the Lamb of God",
Volume 33, Sermon #1987 - John 1:29

False doctrines cannot be proved, and you need not make the attempt. It is only the truth which is capable of proof.

"As We Have Heard, So Have We Seen",
Volume 34, Sermon #2014 - Psalm 48:8

Error is multiform; truth is one. A thousand lies will live together, and tolerate each other, especially at this time, when errorists are all crying out, "Cast in thy lot with us; let us all have one purse."

Jesus Known By Personal Revelation,
Volume 34, Sermon #2041 - Matthew 16:13-17

Men cannot see truth, because they love falsehood. The gospel is not seen, because it is too pure for their loose lives and lewd thoughts.

The Eye and the Light,
Volume 35, Sermon #2109 - Luke 11:33-36

Every precious thing in this world is sure to be counterfeited.

The Peace of the Devil and the Peace of God,
Volume 36, Sermon #2157 - Luke 11:21, Psalm 29:11

A man's mind is rich very much in proportion to the truth he knows.

The Believer's Heritage of Joy,
Volume 41, Sermon #2415 - Psalm 119:111

Some people say, "Why, you are in such a small minority!" Yes, yes; but as a general rule minorities are right. Up until now, the majority has never been on the side of Christ, the majority has never been for God, the majority has never been with the truth.

Converts, and Their Confession of Faith,
Volume 41, Sermon #2429 - Isaiah 44:5

The truth is as old as the everlasting hills. Therefore, dear friends, be not touched with that Athenian madness of always seeking after some new thing. Did you ever hear of new gold? to all intents and purposes, all gold that is worth having is old.

Place for the Word,
Volume 44, Sermon #2584 - John 8:37

I would not give a penny for your love to the truth if it is not accompanied with a hearty hatred of error.

Open Praise and Public Confession,
Volume 45, Sermon #2604 - Psalm 138:1-3

One man abiding in the truth has more weight in his witness than millions under the power of the father of lies.

Positivism,
Volume 55, Sermon #3161 - 1 John 5:18-20

Only give truth time, and, God being with her, she must prevail. 3

Discipline in Christ's Army,
Volume 56, Sermon #3188 - Joshua 1:11

It is a strange thing that if the old evangelistic doctrines should appear for one moment to be beaten in debate, they always conquer in results.

Christ and His Hearers,
Volume 60, Sermon #3410 - Luke 15:1, 2

Unbelief

We often talk of unbelief as if it were an affliction to be pitied instead of a crime to be condemned.

An All Around Ministry, Page 136

The first step astray is a want of adequate faith in the divine inspiration of the Sacred Scriptures.

The Down Grade Controversy, Page 13

The angels never doubt Him, nor the devils either; we alone, out of all the beings that God has fashioned, dishonor Him by unbelief, and tarnish His honor by mistrust.

Morning and Evening, Page 629

This would be the first step in apostasy; men first forget the true, and then adore the false.

The Treasury of David, Psalm 44, Verse 20

Even if a man had no other sin whatsoever, it is quite sufficient to condemn him for ever, that he neglects his God and turns away from his Savior; for unbelief is an act of high treason against the divine majesty, plucking at the crown jewel of Jehovah's truthfulness.

Forts Demolished An Prisoners Taken,
Volume 25, Sermon #1473 - 2 Corinthians 10:5

It seems to me that an angel, looking down upon a sinner who has rejected Christ, will think of him as some sevenfold atrocity of nature.

Mocking the King,
Volume 55, Sermon #3138 - Matthew 27:28-30

Will of God

We read in Scripture of several instances where God apparently changed, but I think the observation of the old Puritan explains all these; he says, "God may will a change, but he cannot change his will."

What God Cannot Do!,
Volume 10, Sermon #568 - Titus 1:2

It is nothing but wickedness, whatever form it assumes, when we attempt to resist the will of God.

"This Thing Is From Me",
Volume 42, Sermon #2476 - 1 Kings 12:24

If there is anything about the Lord's will that you do not like, my dear Brothers and Sisters, that is a point in which you are wrong!

Honor for Honor,
Volume 50, Sermon #2906 - 1 Samuel 2:30

You cannot say that Jesus Christ ever troubled His head about what He should eat, or what He should drink—His meat and His drink consisted in doing His Father's will!

Thought Condemned, Yet Commanded,
Volume 52, Sermon #2973 - Matthew 6:31-33

Infinite wisdom dictates what absolute sovereignty decrees. God is never arbitrary, or tyrannical. He does as he wills, but he always wills to do that which is not only most for his own glory, but also most for our real good. How dare we question anything God does?

Fifteen Years After!,
Volume 53, Sermon #3025 - Job 1:21

Even if we do not always use the words, "If the Lord wills," "If God pleases," "If we are spared," or similar expressions, let the spirit of them always be in our mind so that we do not think and speak unconditionally concerning the unknown future!

Maroth-Or, the Disappointed,
Volume 56, Sermon #3184 - Micah 1:12

Obedience to the will of God is the pathway to perpetual honor and everlasting joy!

The Priesthood of Believers,
Volume 57, Sermon #3266 - 1 Peter 2:5

Wisdom

The doorstep of the palace of wisdom is a humble sense of ignorance.

Barbed Arrows, Page 280

Truly wise men are never above asking questions, because they are wise men.

Christ's Incarnation, Page 98

True religion is sanctified common sense. Attention to the things of heaven does not necessitate the neglect of the affairs of earth; on the contrary, he who has learned how to transact business with God ought to be best able to do business with men.

The Treasury of David, Psalm 112, Verse 5

If you have not the time, God gave it to you, and you must have misspent it.

A Bad Excuse Is Worse Than None,
Volume 10, Sermon #578 - Luke 14:18

Wisdom is, I suppose, the right use of knowledge. To know is not to be wise. Many men know a great deal, and are all the more fools for what they know. There is no fool so great a fool as a knowing fool.

The Fourfold Treasure,
Volume 17, Sermon #991 - 2 Corinthians 1:30,31

Our Creator is infinitely good, and his will is love: to submit to one who is "to wise to err, too good to be unkind," should not be hard.

Unconditional Surrender,
Volume 22, Sermon #1276 - James 4:7

Many a man might have known if he had but been aware that he did not know. A sense of ignorance is the doorstep of the palace of wisdom.

Teaching for the Outer and Inner Circles,
Volume 28, Sermon #1669 - Mark 4:33, 34

Always have something in hand that is greater than your present capacity.

The Necessity of Growing Faith,
Volume 31, Sermon #1857 - 2 Thessalonians 1:3

Do not be ashamed of confessing your past folly. I think a man who says, "I was wrong," really in effect says, "I am a little wiser to-day than I was yesterday."

How Faith Comes,
Volume 45, Sermon #2623 - John 4:39-42

I will give you a little bit of worldly wisdom; it is this,—whenever you do not know what to do, do not do it.

Two Choice Assurances,
Volume 58, Sermon #3330 - Genesis 15:1, Exodus 33:14

Wives

She is a wicked wife who drives her husband away by her long tongue.

John Ploughman's Talk, Page 94

God save us all from wives who are angels in the streets, saints in the church, and devils at home.

John Ploughman's Talk, Page 95

You are as much serving God in looking after your own children, and training them up in God's fear, and minding the house, and making your household a church for God, as you would be if you had been called to lead an army to battle for the Lord of hosts.

Strengthening Medicine for God's Servants,
Volume 21, Sermon #1214 - Joshua 1:5

Work

God has not one single servant for whom He has not appointed a service.

A Good Start, Page 74

Never set a man to work he is not fit for, for he will never do it well.

John Ploughman's Pictures, Page 32

Work is always healthier for us than idleness; it is always better to wear out shoes than sheets.

John Ploughman's Talk, Page 128

He who undertakes too much succeeds but little.

John Ploughman's Talk, Page 140

You may burst a bag by trying to fill it too full, and ruin yourself by grasping at too much.

John Ploughman's Talk, Page 140

There's no shame about any honest calling; don't be afraid of soiling your hands, there's plenty of soap to be had.

John Ploughman's Talk, Page 142

God sends every bird its food, but he does not throw it into the nest: he gives us our daily bread, but it is through our own labour.

John Ploughman's Talk, Page 143

We are not saved by service, but we are saved to service.

We Endeavor, Page 6

We serve God or the devil in all that we do.

A Well-Ordered Life,
Volume 15, Sermon #878 - Psalm 119:133

Man was not made for an idle life, labour is evidently his proper condition. Even when man was perfect he was placed in the garden, not to admire its flowers, but to keep it and to dress it. If he needed to work when he was perfect, much more does he require the discipline of labour now that he is fallen.

One Lion, Two Lions, No Lion At All!,
Volume 28, Sermon #1670 - Proverbs 22:13; 26:13

I would rather create an ounce of help than a ton of theory.

The Blind Man's Eyes Opened-Or, Practical Christianity,
Volume 29, Sermon #1754 - John 9:3, 4

Amongst the sanitary and salutary regulations of the moral universe there is none much better than this—that men must work.

The Hedge of Thorns and the Plain Way,
Volume 33, Sermon #1948 - Proverbs 15:19

Surely you have some natural faculty or acquired skill which you can lay at his feet.

"David's Spoil",
Volume 34, Sermon #2017 - 1 Samuel 30:20

Our endeavors to go up lead us to push others down.

The Iniquity of Our Holy Things,
Volume 36, Sermon #2153 - Exodus 28:36-38

We should work with the hands of Martha, but yet keep near the Master with the heart of Mary; we want a combination of activity and meditation.

Faithful Stewardship,
Volume 41, Sermon #2440 - 1 Corinthians 4:2

A man is never perfectly at peace if he is ambitious, and craving for this or that which as yet is beyond his reach.

"Peace in Believing",
Volume 45, Sermon #2626 - Romans 15:13

Take care, Christian workers, that in this day of activity, when there is so much to do, you do not neglect the personal act of faith which unites your soul to Christ. See to this vital and all-important matter.

The Search Warrant,
Volume 50, Sermon #2898 - John 6:64

The more work we have to do with men for God, the longer we ought to be at work with God for men. If you plead with men, you cannot hope to prevail unless you first plead with God.

A Lift for the Prostrate,
Volume 52, Sermon #2980 - Mark 1:31

Albeit we are not saved by works, yet the ultimate result of salvation must always be work. The cause of salvation lies in Grace, but the effect of salvation appears in working. As sure as ever the Grace of God fills a soul, that soul desires to see others brought in.

God's Glory in the Building Up of Zion,
Volume 55, Sermon #3147 - Psalm 102:16

The true worker is not to be blamed that as yet there are no fruits, but he is to be blamed if he is content always to be without fruits.

Joy in Harvest,
Volume 58, Sermon #3315 - Isaiah 9:3

The World

What would be the worth of the opinions of all the men in the world as to the state of a soul before God?

Soul Satisfaction,
Volume 55, Sermon #3137 - Psalm 35:3

If there is a religion concerning which all men speak well, woe be unto it, for it cannot be the religion of Christ!

Secret Disciples Encouraged,
Volume 56, Sermon #3207 - John 18:25

Those whom no man can pity and no man can help, God can love and save!

God in Heaven, and Men on the Sea,
Volume 58, Sermon #3321 - Psalm 65:5

Actual sermon manuscript amended by Spurgeon.

For authentic, high-quality Spurgeon manuscripts, please visit www.raredoctraders.com

This book was partially funded in memory of Amy Horton.

In college, Amy and I were blessed by being part of a group called the Dead Preacher's Society, which met each weekday afternoon to read a sermon, most of which were by Charles Spurgeon. As we grew in love for each other, we also grew in love for the Christ that Spurgeon preached so clearly and fully.

In the spring of 2011, Amy was diagnosed with colon cancer while pregnant with our third child. The baby was born healthy, but Amy's cancer was both advanced and aggressive. She passed away on June 5, 2012, at the age of thirty-one in the assurance that Christ would own her for eternity.

A donation was made to this work in her memory in the hope that the blessing we received through the writing of Charles Spurgeon would overflow to others and that some may start their own practice of reading his sermons together.

Tyler Horton

Through the Eyes of C. H. Spurgeon

ABOUT THE EDITOR

I am a follower of Jesus Christ, a husband to Samantha, and a dad to Micah. I live in central Canada, serve in my local church and am the sole proprietor of www.throughtheeyesofspurgeon.com. Connect with me on Facebook (www.facebook.com/stephenmccaskell) or by email (stephen@throughtheeyesofspurgeon.com).

Grace and peace be with you all as you seek, serve, and love in the name of our Master, our Friend, and our Savior, Jesus Christ.

– Stephen McCaskell